Praise for *Us vs. Them*

"The biggest challenge facing businesses today is generational differences. We either learn how to work with each other, or we can close the doors. Jeff Havens has nailed the problem, the challenges, the frustrations, and has the fixes to work through them. Your business can't survive without this information."

—**Larry Winget**, six time *New York Times/Wall Street Journal* best-selling author, social commentator, and television personality. Author of *Grow a Pair: How to Stop Being a Victim* and *Take Back Your Life, Your Business, and Your Sanity*

"With a dash of wit, pinch of irreverence, helping of data and analysis, sprinkle of snark, and hint of anecdotal flavor, Jeff Havens has provided a straightforward set of strategies that supports a clear pathway of understanding and success for all in the workplace. *Us vs. Them* is the perfect antidote to the Me vs. You syndrome and delivers a framework where we all really can just get along and thrive in the workplace."

—**Cindy Cisneros**, Vice President of Education Programs, Committee for Economic Development

"In *Us vs. Them*, Jeff Havens helps bridge generational gaps with his witty insight in this hilarious, helpful, and refreshing book."

—**Ashley Rhodes-Courter, MSW**, International and *New York Times* best-selling author of *Three Little Word* and *Three More Words*

"In his book, Jeff Havens provides supervisors with much simpler guidelines than the current, more complicated literature on generations. *Us vs. Them* makes sense! It also avoids the negative messages that some generational literature presents. It delivers strategies and easy low-cost to no-cost ideas that will really work."

—**Angela S. Kemp, SPHR & GPHR**, 32-year HR and communications professional

"Multi-Generational Workplaces may sound like the name of a Seattle grunge band, but once you read *Us vs. Them*, you'll be the one holding the drumsticks."

—**Tim McEachern**, co-author, *The New, New Economy*

"*Us vs. Them* covers a very important topic for our management team. We have developed a class specifically on this topic and the ideas I am getting from this book will prove invaluable in training our managers. I find Jeff's approach to this subject very refreshing as he uses real world examples that everyone can relate to."

—**Johnny Carcioppolo**, Director, Corporate Learning Solutions, Jack Henry & Associates, Inc.®

"Jeff's book is written in a light-hearted and conversational tone, which makes it easy and enjoyable to read. It's like sitting at the kitchen table with a friend having a chat about practical ways to work and how to get along with lots of people. His examples are real, and his suggestions are down to earth and applicable to anyone, no matter what their background."

—**Becky Ropp**, Director, Talent Management, GROWMARK, Inc.

"Jeff Havens is, in a word: freaking hilarious...ok, two. Seriously, not many writers can make me laugh out loud, but this guy is SERIOUSLY funny. In *Us vs. Them* Jeff cleverly weaves insightful real life case studies about loyalty, work ethic, mentorship, complacency, innovation, and change, with sprinkles of Yoda-like generational wisdom that are designed to help you achieve greater results in business, as well as in life. If you're managing people, hiring people, or are looking to get hired—this book is a must-read. Trust me, the footnotes alone are worth the price of admission!"

—**Ross Bernstein**, best-selling sports author and award-winning business speaker

"In the workplace there are still minefields to conquer, language to temper, and management styles to avoid. Luckily, you've got Jeff Havens as your tour guide, and he takes his readers on an entertaining and intergenerational journey of how to make work a little less painful, a lot more profitable, and maybe even fun."

—**Steve Culbertson**, CEO, Youth Service America

Us vs. Them

Us vs. Them

Redefining the Multi-Generational Workplace to Inspire Your Employees to Love Your Company, Drive Innovation, and Embrace Change

Jeff Havens

Publisher: Paul Boger
Editor-in-Chief: Amy Neidlinger
Executive Editor: Jeanne Glasser Levine
Cover Designer: Chuti Prasertsith
Managing Editor: Kristy Hart
Project Editor: Andy Beaster
Copy Editor: Kitty Wilson
Indexer: Lisa Stumpf
Proofreader: Language Logistics, LLC
Compositor: Nonie Ratcliff
Manufacturing Buyer: Dan Uhrig

© 2015 by Jeff Havens
Pearson Education, Inc.
Old Tappan, New Jersey 07675

For information about buying this title in bulk quantities, or for special sales opportunities (which may include electronic versions; custom cover designs; and content particular to your business, training goals, marketing focus, or branding interests), please contact our corporate sales department at corpsales@pearsoned.com or (800) 382-3419.

For government sales inquiries, please contact governmentsales@pearsoned.com.

For questions about sales outside the U.S., please contact international@pearsoned.com.

Company and product names mentioned herein are the trademarks or registered trademarks of their respective owners.

Printed in the United States of America

First Printing June 2015

ISBN-10: 0-13-419510-8
ISBN-13: 978-0-13-419510-0

Pearson Education LTD.
Pearson Education Australia PTY, Limited.
Pearson Education Singapore, Pte. Ltd.
Pearson Education Asia, Ltd.
Pearson Education Canada, Ltd.
Pearson Educacion de Mexico, S.A. de C.V.
Pearson Education—Japan
Pearson Education Malaysia, Pte. Ltd.

Library of Congress Control Number: 2015936807

To Occam and his glorious razor

Contents

Acknowledgments

The author of any book owes a debt of gratitude to a number of people. In my case, dozens of personal and professional acquaintances helped me with the stories that populate *Us vs. Them*. However, as they were promised anonymity in exchange for their unvarnished honesty, I'll have to settle for thanking them poorly here and more properly the next time we get together for a drink and (if they were really nice to me) an appetizer combo. I'd also like to thank everyone at the Bureau of Labor Statistics for painstakingly compiling decades of workplace data that has turned out to have some quite surprising information. A special thanks to Robin Dunbar, whose fascinating research is especially incredible because almost nobody seems to know about it. And while I'm at it, I feel I should thank all those folks who built the Internet. I've found it to be somewhat helpful.

About the Author

Jeff Havens has spoken to hundreds of companies and associations on issues of generational tension, leadership, communication, and change management. A Phi Beta Kappa graduate of Vanderbilt University, he has also worked as a teacher, stand-up comedian, and street performer. The author of several books, he lives in Michigan with his wife, Laura, and their dog, Pancake. For more information, visit www.jeffhavens.com.

Introduction: Why This Book Needed to Be Written

Greetings and congratulations! By choosing to buy or steal this book, you have made an incredible decision, one that is going to help you address some of the most fundamental issues currently affecting your professional life. In a few short chapters, we discuss all of the following:

- How to more effectively motivate your youngest employees to avoid high turnover

- How to prevent your oldest employees from coasting their way into retirement

- Why your career might not be advancing as fast as you think it should and what you can do about it

- How to frame changes to your business in language that everyone can understand and get on board with

- Why many of your colleagues think differently than you and what you can learn from them

- How to build and maintain a corporate culture that will inspire enthusiasm, loyalty, and a higher level of productivity from *everyone*

This is a book for professionals at every level: managers, employees, young workers, older workers, C-suite executives, students of business management and human resources, and even jobseekers. It might even help parents understand their children better—and vice versa. If you've ever had problems with people who were either significantly older or younger than you, this book is going to make your life happier and easier.

But maybe you haven't bought or stolen this book yet. Maybe you're standing just outside an airport bookstore, suitcase in one hand and a bagel sandwich in your mouth while you search for something to help you kill time until you can finally board your next flight. If that's the case, then at this point you might be wondering, "Why should I buy this book? Why should I even bother stealing it? I've already read a few books about generational issues at work. How is this one going to be any different?"

Those are great questions, and I'm glad you hypothetically asked. There are indeed thousands of books on generational issues. So how is this book different? Because the current prevailing conversation about generational issues in the workplace is a needlessly complicated and profoundly *un*helpful way to look at the subject. The goal of this book is twofold: first, to undo several decades of bad practice regarding generational differences in the workplace; second, to put the generational issues you're currently facing into a simple framework that will remain eminently sensible, immediately actionable, and relentlessly relevant for the rest of your life. We don't talk about how to "manage Millennials" or "get along with your Boomer bosses." We discuss strategies that will help you resolve *every* generational issue you will *ever* face. That's what this book is going to do.

But first, let me take a step back. I've been using the word *book* to describe what you're reading, but I realize that might not be the right word. It's possible that you're holding an actual book, and if you are, it's most likely because you like the feel of a real book or because nobody has ever bought you an e-reader.

It's also possible, however, that you're reading this on your tablet, or on your phone, or on the computer monitor that has recently been implanted in your eyeball. If that's the case, I'm sorry for using the word *book* so often. In case you don't know, they were kind of like papyrus scrolls that didn't need to be rolled up when you finished. You might have accidentally seen one in the mall on your way to the Apple store. Indeed, it's largely because I don't know how you're looking at these words that these words needed to be written.

Now ordinarily this would be the part of a book about generational issues where I should say something like, "The world of today is a lot different than it used to be." I'm fairly certain you've heard this sentence a hundred thousand times. And on the surface, it almost sounds like a useful thing to say. After all, when I grew up, there were approximately 12 channels of television,[1] and if you wanted to call someone on the phone you had to actually know his or her phone number. How anyone ever got hold of anybody is a total mystery. Now the entire corpus of human knowledge is in your pocket wherever you go, and you can become a millionaire by making weird movies alone in your basement.

So obviously things are different now, and that's what I'm supposed to tell you right here. Then I'm supposed to point out that those differences are causing you to ask questions you never thought you would have to ask yourself—questions such as

- How do I inspire loyalty in my employees when the very idea of employee loyalty seems to no longer exist?

- How long can my current business model survive when things seem to be changing literally every second?

- Are young people today really less motivated than they were in my time, or am I being unfair?

- Why do some people insist on sticking with outdated practices when there are new and better things coming out every day?

There are just three problems with that approach. First, the "things are different now" argument is implicitly speaking *to* older workers *about* younger workers. In fact, that's what most books about generational issues do, which is why most books about generational issues are really, really annoying.

---

[1] Along with a U channel that never seemed to do anything. Why were you there, U? What was your dark and mysterious purpose?

Summary of Far Too Many Generational Books, Keynotes, and Articles

"Today's young people are different. Deal with it."

Predictably, this "message" only serves to make every older person even more resistant to the idea of looking at the world from another point of view because there is absolutely no hint of a compromise. I've sat in on those talks before and listened to multiple audience members say some version of the following: "Why should I have to be the only one making any changes? *I'm* employing *them*; why don't *they* have to deal with the way *I* like to do things?" Which, by the way, is exactly how you should feel when the message you're receiving is "Deal with it."

Resolving generational differences will never, *never* work if any one group of people feel like they're the only ones who have to make any concessions.[2]

The second problem with this approach is that the "things are different now" argument is wildly misleading, albeit unintentionally so. By saying things are different *now*, there is the implication that what we're experiencing today is somehow unique in human history, that this is the *first* time things have truly been different from one generation to the next. But that simply isn't true. The rise of computers and the Internet is the defining difference of our time. They have presented us with a massive shift in the way the world operates, and we talk throughout this book about the different effects that the Internet in particular, and our technological revolution in general, have had on the people who established themselves before their advent and those who were born and raised entirely under their influence. But the fact of something new coming along and creating a schism between people of different ages is a fairly common occurrence. You could

---

[2] And just in case you doubt the truth of this statement, go tell your spouse that from now on you're done listening to his or her thoughts and ideas. You are no longer going to make any concessions to his or her feelings and aspirations because from now on your word is law. Give it a shot! I'll buy you a drink when you get kicked out.

say the same for the British Invasion and its effect on generational attitudes in the 1960s, the automobile and its effect on people during the Gilded Age, or the printing press and how it polarized Europeans in the late 1400s. Simply saying "things are different now" doesn't help resolve anything because the differences we're facing now aren't affecting generational tensions in a fundamentally distinct way from what has happened multiple times in the past.

And the third problem, which is related to the second, is that the questions you're probably asking yourself today—Why do your younger colleagues seem to be so capricious and disloyal? Why do some of your older colleagues seem so stuck in their ways? and so on—are the same questions people have always asked. In almost every way, the generational issues you're facing today are the same issues that have plagued the professional world for centuries. The vast majority of today's conversation about generational issues encourages the attitude that the problems you're dealing with are novel and therefore require novel solutions. For years you've been told that there are four teams competing against each other, that we have somehow evolved into a *multi*generational workplace. But that simply *isn't true.* It isn't true now, and it's never been that way. Since the dawn of civilization, there have only ever been two generations. It's always been Us vs. Them.

Fundamentally, our world is a world of human beings and the interactions between us. Throughout all of recorded human history, technology has always changed things, and so have political decisions and local economics and global trade and cultural attitudes. It's important to understand what today's issues are so that we can address them with the right tools instead of trying to solve today's problems with strategies and attitudes that are designed for the world of 50 or 100 or 3,000 years ago. For that reason, a portion of our discussion will focus on computers and the Internet and 24/7 media and the various effects those institutions have had.

But those discussions will be a minority of what this book is. If you want to successfully navigate the world today, tomorrow, or at any other time in your life, the most important thing to do is not to understand *what* the issues are but rather *why* the people around you are acting and reacting the way they are. Fortunately, those answers are rooted in basic human psychology, which has done us the favor of staying more or less constant since our cave-dwelling days. So by the end of this book, I guarantee that you will know *everything* you need to know in order to understand the different motivations of *everyone* you work with, whether they're 18 or 88. That might sound like a bold statement, and it is. But as you'll see, there aren't many differences that separate us from one another. So if you want to have happier, healthier, more productive relationships with *everyone* you work with—and if you want to have a happier, healthier, and more productive career as a result—then this book will give you exactly what you need.

To put this another way: Most generational books make the issue more complicated than it needs to be, and *Us vs. Them* will make it simple again.

However, I realize that parts of this book come dangerously close to reading like a treatise, and I certainly don't want to bore you. Those of you who have seen my keynote presentations, read my other books, or participated in our various training programs know that I always make a particular effort to be as entertaining as possible, and so I promise I'll be doing the same in this book. You'll end up getting a lot of answers, but you'll also get to laugh while you read this. I know it's not supposed to be that way; you're *supposed* to read this book because somebody gave it to you or because you want to impress your boss or because every so often you have trouble getting to sleep and business books are often better than Valium or cyanide or whatever pill you usually take at night. But I figured you might forgive me if I decided to do everything possible to make this discussion as entertaining as possible. I'm doing this in part because of a recent groundbreaking survey, which discovered that people enjoy fun things more than boring things.

So let's first prove that you actually do have some issues with people from a different generation than your own because you might be reading this and thinking, "I admit that there are generational tensions where I work, but I don't personally harbor any negative stereotypes about people from different generations than my own. I am a paragon of objectivity."

If this describes you, then let me just say two things: First, I doubt you thought the word *paragon*. And second, you're a big fat liar. And I will prove it to you with a pair of thought experiments.

Thought Experiment #1: Proof That You Do Indeed Harbor Stereotypes About Different Generations

I want you to imagine that you're a parent. You have a son and daughter, both in the single digits, and it's bedtime. At least, *you* think it's bedtime. Your son and daughter, however, have a different idea. They don't want to go to bed, and they're making their disagreement known. You have a conundrum on your hands, a generational difference of opinion. What do you do?

A. You sit your kids down and have a long, rational, calm, and quiet conversation about the merits of an early bedtime. You listen patiently to your children's arguments, validating their ideas with phrases such as, "I see what you're saying," and "That's an interesting perspective." You each write down your needs on separate sheets of paper, along with potential solutions to the issue, then compare notes to find where your ideas overlap. Then, with a firm desire for collaboration and mutual happiness established on both sides, you find a compromise that leaves both parties feeling like they've been heard. Happiness reigns forever, and the argument about when bedtime should occur immediately disappears from your family discourse.

B. Taking your cues from the stock market, you treat the issue like a matter of shareholder debate. You assign shares to each family member based on their financial contribution to the whole family enterprise. When your kids protest that federal labor laws prohibit them from working, you agree to assign them household chores that will serve as their contribution. After tense negotiations about the relative pay due for services such as cleaning their rooms and putting their dishes in the dishwasher, you convene a shareholder meeting where objections and ideas can be heard. Eventually the issue is put to a vote, and all parties agree to abide by the outcome of that vote until the next shareholder meeting, which will occur in three months (as per your charter) or as changing conditions merit.

C. You shove your kids in their footie pajamas and throw them in bed. You know you can't reason with them, so you don't even try. They'll probably whine and cry about it, but who cares if they cry? It'll just make them tired, and they won't remember it in the morning anyway.

So, which one did you pick? Oh, wait, *that was a trick question!!!!* Because I know you chose C. It's the only choice that makes any sense. And although I'll admit you probably don't treat your younger colleagues and employees in quite this fashion, I'm also confident you have occasionally viewed them and their ideas with varying levels of dismissal and disbelief.

But wait—there's more!

Thought Experiment #2: Proof That You Do Indeed Harbor Stereotypes About Different Generations

You're in a grocery store, and you're stocking up on everything. It's late at night, and there's only one checkout lane open. There is a do-it-yourself lane, but you have a lot of produce that doesn't have barcodes on it, and you don't want to scroll through that stupid digital menu to find 16 different prices. However, as you're wheeling your overflowing cart into the line, you see an elderly gentleman in front of you. He's just set his groceries on the conveyor belt, and just as you're wondering why he's not already in bed, you see him pull a checkbook out of his jacket pocket. You realize with horror that the poor old man still thinks it's 1956. What do you do?

A. You wait patiently behind him, realizing that different people do things in different ways and that none of them is better than any other. At some point during your wait, you experience a moment of poignant nostalgia for simpler days, when everyone paid with checks and bagboys escorted everyone to their cars and America was unquestionably ascendant. When he finishes paying, you thank him for the trip down memory lane and offer to walk him to his car so you can put his groceries in the trunk for him. He thanks you for the service, and you then return inside to pay for your own groceries, imbued with a sense of civic pride.

B. You have a brief, informative conversation with him about the ease and utility of debit cards. He expresses wonderment and then fear because he just doesn't know if he can trust the bank not to steal from him; after all, he's been reading a lot lately about people getting their passwords stolen. Understanding his concern, you invite him to an early lunch where you show him the various security protocols that banks use to ensure that their customers' money is well protected, and you also provide him hard copies of several independent reviews of debit cards to help put his mind at ease. You then provide him with some basic financial planning, putting him on a sound financial footing for retirement before recommending to him a trusted professional. He thanks you by offering to set you up with his neighbor's grandchild.

C. You go to the do-it-yourself lane so you can get home before bedtime. Seriously, why are old people always so slow?! They don't have as much time left, so why aren't they in a hurry? But they're not, are they? *They never are!!!!*

And the winner is C again! You know what you would do in that situation probably because you've almost certainly been in that position already. And again, I've hyperbolized because it's entertaining to do so, but I'm certain you've experienced some amount of frustration with the speed, style, and sheer stubbornness of your older colleagues and employees.

Here, in a nutshell, is what you're going to find in *Us vs. Them:*

- We begin by destroying once and for all the four-generation model and replace it with an easier and more intuitive two-generation model.

- You learn to which generation you belong, as well as the common stereotypes each generation harbors about the other.

- We then discuss each of those stereotypes in turn, focusing specifically on *why* each generation thinks and behaves the way it does and how that knowledge will help you construct a true compromise between both generations that everyone will not only understand but also agree is a workable strategy.

I want to thank you for choosing to read this book. It's becoming something of an obsession of mine to simplify the current confusion revolving around generational issues in the workplace. We sometimes like to make things more difficult than they need to be, and doing so is rarely in our best interests. So I'm hopeful you'll walk away from *Us vs. Them* with an approach to your own generational tensions at work that will be profoundly and permanently successful.

So what are you waiting for? Turn the page or swipe left or do a downscroll eyeblink, and let's get going!

Part One
Simplifying the Picture

1

Destroying the Four-Generation Myth

You're forgiven if you've gotten tired of hearing about generational issues in the workplace. Amazon lists more than 1,100 books with the words *generation* and *workplace* in the title. That's the equivalent of a new book on generational issues in the workplace being published every 6½ days for the past 20 years. If you're fatigued, it's because you should be. Talking about the same issue in the same way and with the same language over and over and over again is exhausting.

Indeed, it's precisely because of this avalanche of literature that I've been compelled to write this book. The way we have been thinking about generational differences in the past two decades—the central premise behind those 1,100 books and the uncountable others with cleverer titles that talk about the same thing—is making it harder for us to find workable solutions. We've been complicating the problem rather than solving it.

Fortunately, things are much easier than they seem.

It's not that there aren't significant differences between generations; there are. For example

- You might have grown up listening to record albums—and not as an accoutrement to your retro lifestyle but because it was the only form in which music came. If you did, it's possible you also grew up drinking phosphates, lounging on the davenport, wearing derby hats, and hoarding lamp oil.

- You may never have seen a pay phone. Perhaps you wonder if they were phones that paid you.

- You may have all but forgotten that the English language has vowels and rules for proper spelling, and that thngs r rlly hrdr if u brk th roolz all th tim.

- You might have grown up without the Internet, which necessarily means you spent your entire childhood being bored. What did you do for fun? Nobody knows.
- You might still have a fake ID in your dresser.
- You might have fake teeth sitting on your dresser.
- You might have children who learned things in fifth grade that you yourself didn't learn until high school or college.
- You might be worried about your pension.
- You might not be quite certain what a pension is—or, more accurately, what a pension *was*.

It's a safe bet that some of these descriptions remind you of you, and some of them make you shake your head at the people to whom those descriptions apply. We are undoubtedly different. But we've allowed ourselves to categorize those differences in a thoroughly unhelpful way. We take as axiomatic the following sentence:

For the first time in history, there are four distinct generations operating side by side.

Every speaker, book, lecture, infographic, or TED talk that addresses generational issues is founded on the premise of this four-generation workplace. It's so ubiquitous that you've probably never questioned it. Instead, you've asked yourself, "How am I supposed to get anything done when there are so many people with so many different needs, motivations, desires, goals, and issues? How can I balance all these conflicting desires against each other in a way that works for everyone and somehow doesn't consume my every waking thought?"

Again, if you have ever felt overwhelmed by the multigenerational workplace, it's not your fault. You've simply been persuaded by an endless stream of "generational experts" telling you how crazy and difficult and unprecedented the working world is today. In fact, some of them *want* you to feel overwhelmed. They *want* you to be scared. That's how they sell you things: by making these issues seem bigger than they really are and then offering "solutions" to those artificially inflated problems.

But not me. I don't want you to be scared, except maybe of sharks and botulism and close talkers and other things it makes sense to be scared of. When it comes to your career, however, I want you to feel secure. The challenges facing today's workforce are not unprecedented. In many ways, they are the same challenges that have been facing professionals for centuries.

The point of this chapter is to banish once and for all the notion that there are four generations in today's workplace. The four-generation model is entirely unworkable if you want to create loyalty, dedication, and runaway success. Thinking of your workforce as multigenerational creates more problems than it solves. Fortunately for us, there are *not* four generations operating side by side. That's a lie whose time has come, and this book is going to bury it once and for all.

Generational Differences Throughout the Ages

Strictly speaking, the length of a *generation* is the amount of time it takes for an infant to get old enough to have children of his or her own. Historically this has ranged anywhere from around 13 years (please don't have kids when you're 13, by the way) up to 40 years—although it's hard to say exactly how our ancestors measured the length of a generation because there's decent evidence to suggest that nobody paid it even the slightest amount of attention. I've typed every possible permutation of "generational differences" into every search engine there is,[1] and there are exactly *zero* mentions of generational differences being an issue that anyone talked about in any form whatsoever before about 1960.

This means that for the majority of human history, generational differences either didn't exist (which is seriously unlikely) or were framed in different terms (which we'll be discussing in greater detail shortly).

---

[1] Except Bing. But I'm not counting that against me.

The most common argument used to explain why we have a four-generation workforce for the first time in human history is that—you know what's coming, don't you?—the world today is different than it used to be. These are the two platitudes we always trot out when discussing generational issues: *For the first time in history, there are four distinct generations operating side by side, and the world today is different than it used to be.* But let's put this into a proper perspective. The Revolutionary War was as comprehensive and world-altering for early Americans as WWII was for the so-called Silent Generation; the French and Russian revolutions were significantly more volatile and transformative than the 1960s and Vietnam were for the Baby Boomers; and the printing press was easily as colossal a technological innovation for 15th- and 16th-century Europeans as the Internet has been for today's Generations X and Y (and the rest of us, too). There is nothing so unique about our world today that we can't find parallels from earlier eras. And yet our ancestors didn't talk about the travails of negotiating a multigenerational workforce, and we do.

To be sure, people tended not to live as long as we do today (yay for toilets and medicine and antibacterial soap!), so there would have been fewer instances of 20-year-olds working alongside 40- and 60- and 80-year-olds. But it certainly happened. For example, the 56 signers of the Declaration of Independence ranged in age from 26 (Edward Rutledge, South Carolina) to 70 (Benjamin Franklin, Pennsylvania). In addition to them, there were 2 other signers in their 20s, 17 in their 30s, 21 in their 40s, 8 in their 50s, and 6 in their 60s. By today's measure, these men would absolutely represent a multigenerational workforce, and yet none of them ever made mention of thinking along those lines, despite the fact that many of them were both business owners and prolific writers. Neither did a single factory owner in the first *200 years* after the start of the Industrial Revolution. No one *ever* talked about a multigenerational workforce—not *once*—until 40 or 50 years ago.

So what happened?

The answer, which will surprise you for only a moment if indeed it surprises you at all, is that we have changed the way we market ourselves. Over the past several decades, marketers have systematically worked to create a hyper-complicated picture of our generational differences, specifically so that they could sell "solutions" in the form of books, products and consulting, and a host of other services.[2] Today's "multigenerational workforce" is not a *real* issue; it's a *marketing strategy*. And I'll prove that in the next few pages.

How Marketing Created the "Multigenerational Workforce"

When the Industrial Revolution really got going, it didn't take the producers of goods and services very long to figure out that they needed to have markets in which to sell those goods and services— and the more markets they could find, the more goods and services they'd be able to sell. So they hired marketers to go around inventing new markets.

And those marketers were very, very successful:

- George Frederick Earnshaw, president of Earnshaw Knitting Company in Chicago, published the children's wear industry's first trade journal in 1917, titled *The Infants' Department*. Its aim was to help clothiers increase their sales by targeting infants as a distinct market, which had previously been an ill-defined or non-existent demographic.

- The term *toddler* was coined to describe a distinct demographic around 1936 to distinguish between infants and children— again as a way to sell more clothes.

- In 1997, the book *What Kids Buy: The Psychology of Marketing to Children* identified the *tween* as a demographic distinct from childhood and adolescence and, therefore, a new market

---

[2] By the way, you're totally forgiven right now if you think I'm being hypocritical. After all, I've written a book about this very subject, so maybe you think I'm the same as everyone else. But I promise that's not true. I'm trying to simplify this issue, not add to the confusion. My goal is to make this book the last word on generational issues that you ever have to read. I don't plan on writing another book about generational differences in the workplace because my goal is to ensure that by the end of this, you'll realize that there's really nothing else to say. I want to *kill* the industries that thrive on creating artificial generational differences, not help expand them.

for companies to target. (There's a good chance, by the way, that the word *tween* was first used by J.R.R. Tolkien to describe hobbits. In case you, like me, find that kind of thing interesting.)

I could go on, but you get the point. As recently as a century ago, there were exactly three stages of life: infancy, childhood, and adulthood. Now, we've broken it down something like this:

- **Infant**—0 to 12 or 24 months.
- **Toddler**—1 to 3 years old, according to the CDC
- **Child**—3 to 10-ish years old
- **Tween**—8 to 12 years old (or 10 to 12, depending on the source)
- **Junior teen**—13 to 15 years old
- **Teen**—Technically 13 to 19 years old, but National Miss America says 16 to 18, and other groups have different age ranges
- **Young adult**—10 to 20 years old, or 12 to 18, or 14 to 21, or even 20 to 40 if you go by Erik Erikson's stages of human development

That's *eight* overlapping stages of life, and unless you go by Erik Erikson's definition for *young adult*, we haven't even made it out of college yet. If I kept going with all the stages of adulthood that we've created—young professional, parent, middle-aged, retired, old age, and so on—we'd easily get this list up to 15 categories. Is human life truly five times as complicated and nuanced now as it was a century ago? Or have we segmented ourselves into ever smaller cohorts in order to make it easier to target specific ideas, products, and services to particular populations?

We can also look at music. According to the Music Genres List, there are 23 types of rock music (acid rock, alternative rock, American traditional rock, arena rock, blues rock, British invasion, heavy metal, death metal, hair metal, gothic metal, glam rock, hard rock, noise rock, progressive rock, jam band, psychedelic rock, rock 'n' roll, rockabilly, roots rock, singer/songwriter rock, southern rock, surf rock, and tex-mex). I'm not sure many people would be able to describe the difference between hair metal and glam rock, and yet there are undoubtedly some music aficionados who would be quick to point out that some important genres are missing. And I haven't even mentioned the 12 brands of country, or 16 genres of dance music and 14 flavors of electronic music, nor the fact that inside the alternative rock label there are 9 *further* divisions, each one more and more difficult to distinguish from the others. Dr. M. Duffett, commenting on Simon Reynolds' analysis of indie music for *The Guardian*, puts it very well: "It is as if popular music criticism is now a laboratory which dissects the genetic codes of the tunes in order to guide packs of hungry consumers."

The upshot of our relentless push toward more and more segmentation is that it has the tendency to make *marketing* easier but *living* harder. Take clothing, for example, which is really where this process began. We all know what section to visit in every store or on every website in order to find the things we want, and that's enormously convenient. And at the same time, parents often lament that their children aren't simply *children* anymore; now they belong to subcategories of childhood that seem to be changing on them every time they buy their kids a new outfit. That's worse than inconvenient—it's destructive. Today's children are being placed into categories that didn't exist for the parents who are raising them. Are children magically different today than they were in the 1940s or 1970s? Or are we making things more complicated than they need to be?

So How Does This Relate to the Generational Question?

I have no problem whatsoever with the marketing world's tendency to create finer and finer consumer segments for the purposes of selling products. If a company knows its cameras are extremely popular with 23- to 27-year-old Irish men and creates commercials to attract this audience, that makes perfect sense. If a band bills itself as "countrified acid steampunk with a dash of EBM" and that somehow speaks to their audience, they should do what works.

But people aren't products, and the generational question deals fundamentally with people and the interactions between them. Unfortunately, we've been segmenting various facets of society for marketing purposes for so long (toddler, teen, young professional, and so on) that we've extended the process to people themselves. The term *Baby Boom* was never intended to describe the personality of a generation but rather to indicate the explosion of births following World War II. It wasn't until the 1970s that *Baby Boomer* assumed the connotation it has today; once it did, we became enamored of the belief that every new group of people was somehow fundamentally different than everyone who had come before or who would come after.

Again, this segmentation into Traditionalist, Boomer, Gen X, and Gen Y[3] seems to satisfy our need to understand things. But the more segments we create, the harder it is for us to actually know what we're supposed to do.

There have been several interesting studies about this phenomenon, which for lack of a better term can be called the "poverty of choice." Very basically, the hypothesis goes like this: The more choices we're given, the more indecisive we become, and the more likely we are to do nothing. One of the classic examples of this phenomenon is the famous jam study of 1995.[4] Researchers placed various jams in a display sample at a grocery store. Every few hours, they changed the number of offerings from 6 varieties to 24 varieties. On average, customers tried two samples at both the large and small displays. However, while more people stopped by the larger display (60% at the large display versus 40% at the small display), they made significantly fewer purchases (3% bought something at the large display versus 30% at the smaller display). Several other studies have been conducted with different products and different parameters, but the results tend toward the same conclusion: The more choices we're given, the harder it is for us to know what to do with all those choices.

---

[3] You're now starting to hear some "authorities" describe a new generation, Generation Z, which is distinguished primarily as being "even more technologically oriented" than Generation Y. It seems that as we create more and more generations, we also require fewer and fewer distinctions between one generation and the next. Which begs the question—why are we bothering to create new generations in the first place?

[4] I'll give you a pass if you've never heard of the famous jam study of 1995. It was called the "famous jam study" in the research I found. *Fame*, apparently, is a really, really subjective term.

And this is *exactly* what we've done with the generational question. In creating four distinct generations, we've made our workplaces seemingly *easier* to describe but actually *harder* to manage. If you've ever despaired of figuring out how to work with all the different kinds of people in your office or factory or secret laboratory at the center of the Earth or wherever you work, it's because it feels like a problem too complicated to solve.

But it isn't. We just need to return to thinking about generational issues in a simpler, more natural way—the way all of us did up until a few decades ago.

However, because you've been hearing about four generations since you've been old enough to care about generational issues in the workplace, let's cover what you've heard before.

The Four (Totally Invented) Generations in Today's Workplace

Following is a brief description of each so-called "generation." I've taken the liberty of describing them in slightly different terms than you're used to, but I think you'll agree that my descriptions are not only accurate but also a whole lot more fun than what you're used to reading. Here goes!

Generation #1: The Traditionalists—1922 to 1946

First we have the Traditionalists, also sometimes called The Matures, the Veterans, the WWII Generation, or the Silents. Whatever you decide to call them, they were born roughly between 1922 and 1946, which explains why they make fun of anyone who complains about the state of today's economy. Their favorite medicines growing up were whiskey and cod liver oil, and many of them still maintain the belief that medicine can't possibly be effective if it tastes like anything you would want to put inside you. Seriously, you could get them to eat sand if you told them it would promote their digestive health. They're generally very loyal workers and good rule-followers, and their favorite pastimes are complaining about various physical ailments (often caused by eating too much sand) and yelling at children who run across their lawns, although sadly many of them now live in gated communities and so no longer have lawns to get mad at children for running across. To compensate for this, many of them now yell at their TVs instead. They always drive 18 miles an hour below the speed limit, and they let everyone know that they're turning 7 miles before it's going to happen and about 32 miles after completing the turn. If you've ever been caught behind a Traditionalist driver on the interstate in a single lane of traffic while the other lane is blocked off for the next 23 miles by orange construction cones, then you have a decent idea of what the afterlife is like if you don't make it into Heaven. Traditionalists typically go to bed at 8 p.m., and every year their glasses get a tiny bit thicker. But don't think they're weak! This is the generation who decided three martinis for lunch was a good idea. They can drink the rest of us under the table. Don't underestimate them.

Generation #2: The Baby Boomers—1946 to 1964

Next we have the Baby Boomers—or as I like to call them, the Dirty Filthy Hippies. Born between 1946 and 1964, they were the transitional generation between black-and-white and Technicolor. Instead of whiskey and cod liver oil, their favorite medicine growing up was LSD, which some of them actually tried to get added to our drinking water. They're generally very goal-oriented and sometimes workaholics, which is hard to believe since many of them made it entirely through college without taking a shower. And how can I say that? Because the Baby Boomers were the first group of people since the Vikings to believe that razors and deodorant were somehow part of the oppressive establishment, which means they should have been barred from any decision-making position anywhere. They are notable for their conspicuous consumption and responsible for the absurdly optimistic phrase, "50 is the new 30!" which can be true only if you honestly expect to live to be 134 years old. They invented disco, for which they can never truly be forgiven. And perhaps most importantly, they *also* invented Generations X and Y, although many of them have tried to pretend that they had nothing to do with it.

Generation #3: Generation X—1965 to 1980

After the endless debauchery of the Baby Boomers came Generation X, so named because somewhere in the mid-1970s people apparently ran out of words. This is my generation of people, born between 1965 and 1980. We were famously called the "slacker" generation, which I personally find hilarious considering the generation that comes after us. In a radical departure from our forefathers, our favorite medicine is angst, which isn't even a medicine—it's just a whiny, pouty-faced way of looking at things. Our basic attitude is thus: "Show us your proudest accomplishment, and we'll show you our crushing indifference." We're typically more informal than our elders and have an instinctive distrust for authority, which is hardly a new concept since "distrust of authority" is one of the foundational principles of the American psyche. We're generally described as self-starters, and it's quite evident that we weren't interested in listening to anyone else when we created the fashion sensibilities of the 1980s, which could actually qualify as a crime against humanity. We are the reason for the hole in the ozone layer because we decided it was more important to have big hair than to avoid death by sunburn. Generation X was the first generation in the history of human beings to decide that nobody really understood us, including our friends and family, and that the less people understood us, the cooler we really were. There is really no good explanation for how any Gen Xers survived into adulthood, except that cynicism ultimately isn't fatal. Oh, and we also gave the world rap music. You're welcome.

Generation #4: Generation Y—1980 to Four Minutes Ago

And last but not least—in fact they're the biggest generation in the country, slightly bigger than the Baby Boomers and about twice as large as my mopey Gen Xers—we have Generation Y, so named because by the mid-1990s people were too lazy to even care that X isn't the first letter of the alphabet. They're also known as Millennials—presumably because they were all born on the Millennium Falcon. Born between 1980 and four minutes ago, these people are barely old enough to shave. Their favorite medicine is Ritalin, which has probably been put into their cereal at this point. The proliferation of ADHD diagnoses has happened in large part because this generation, cognizant of the increasing cost of higher education, has chosen to get diagnosed with hyperactivity disorder so that they can pay for college by selling all their extra pills to their friends as "study aids." They're comfortable with new technologies and rapid change because they have never known a time without new technologies and rapid change. This is significant for three reasons. First, it means they've never developed film and been disappointed when 90% of their pictures turned out to be crap. Second, they've never made a mixtape for anyone, painstakingly arranging the songs in the proper order to best express their love for whoever they were going to give it to. And third and perhaps most importantly, they occasionally walk into trees and parked cars and walls and other people when they're texting their friends because they can't be bothered to watch where they're walking. Seriously, they're barely even people.

So there you have the four generations, as I like to think of them. Traditionalists, Boomers, Gen X, and Gen Y. That's what you've heard. That's the only version you've ever heard.

And it's wrong.

The Two Major Problems with the Four-Generation Model

It would be natural to think that these four generational designations make sense. After all, we've been talking about the four-generation workplace for so long that it might be hard to think of it in any other way. You might be saying, "There really do seem to be significant distinctions between each of these groups of people." And you're right: There *are* significant distinctions between people. I'm not saying there aren't. I'm just saying that those differences can be explained in *much* simpler terms than by putting everyone into one of four categories.

And here's why. For one thing, there isn't even much agreement on who belongs in which group. Depending on whom you ask, the Traditionalist Generation begins as early as 1909 or as late as 1925, and it ends sometime between 1940 and 1946. The earliest Baby Boomers were born as early as 1940 or as late as 1946, and they finished up either in 1960 or 1964. Generation Y is *either* the group of people born between 1980 and now, *or* it's a much smaller group (say, between 1979 and the mid-1990s) so that we can apply the unfortunately fashionable Generation Z label to cover anyone born between the mid-1990s and today.

But in terms of imprecision, no "generation" is more obstinately unwilling to be pinned down than Generation X, for whom each of the following explanations has been used:

- Because Generation X is the tenth generation in America (This, by the way, isn't at all true.)
- Because photographer Robert Capa used the term to describe people he was photographing in the 1950s (This means he was actually taking pictures of post-WWII Traditionalists or their Baby Boomer children.)
- Because of Jane Deverson and Charles Hamblett's 1965 book *Generation X* (The authors were certainly interviewing people we would now call Baby Boomers.)
- Because Billy Idol was in a punk band called Generation X in the late 1970s, which was then referenced in Douglas Coupland's *1991* book *Generation X: Tales of an Accelerated Culture*, as the genesis of the term (Huh?)

As you can see, Generation X is a term designed to apply to returning WWII vets, *or* British hippies, *or* Billy Idol, *or* the people we now consider to be Generation X. Even now the best that can be said of Generation X is that they were born sometime in the 1960s and stopped being born (depending on the source) in 1975, 1980, 1981, or 1982.

This is as close to a consensus as we've come, which isn't much of a consensus at all. So the first problem is this: With such fluid designations, how are the millions of people on the edges of a given "generation" supposed to properly self-identify in order to know how to act and interact with others?

The logical counterargument to this criticism is that these years aren't meant to be hard and fast. Instead, they're supposed to function like convenient markers to make sense of the chaos. America didn't suddenly crave independence and decide to go to war in 1776, but we use that year as an easy way to simplify the decades-long process that transformed America from a collection of subservient colonies into its own nation. In the same way, the argument goes, we've picked logical but admittedly arbitrary years to make it easier to talk about the different generations.

But this leads to the second and much, *much* larger problem with the four-generation model. Theoretically, the whole point in having a four-generation model is to make it easier for you to identify and then interact with people from different generations. However, it actually does the opposite. In an effort to justify that there really are significant and fundamental differences between the members of these four "generations," people have created truly exhaustive lists that detail dozens of divergent qualities. I know you've seen those lists before (I'm going to reproduce one for you in couple pages, which I truly, sincerely hope you don't take the time to read), and on most of them there is absolutely no overlap. On the lists where there is some overlap, it's kept to a bare minimum in order to make each generation seem distinct from every other. As a result, the so-called four generations have been presented in a way that makes it look as though the people in each group are rigidly distinct in literally every way imaginable from the people in every other generation—all despite the fact that millions of people hover on the edges of these loosely defined categories and thus might be identified as completely different types of people, depending on which "generation" their age would assign them to.

So here's what you've seen, I'm certain, in every book and keynote presentation about generational issues that you've ever endured. The author or presenter tells you for the millionth time in your life that for the first time in history, there are four distinct generations operating side-by-side in the workplace. He or she then goes on to outline the differences between those "generations." This is the core of the book or presentation, designed to create order out of chaos. After this, you're given various strategies to deal with members of each generation. I'm certain that every one of these authors and presenters is genuinely well intentioned and confident that their advice will be helpful to you. You're then left to take that knowledge and put those strategies into practice. It sounds fairly simple.

But it's not, because the charts they use to delineate their four-generation model make the entire picture too complicated for their well-intentioned advice to have any practical effect.

I'm going to give you one of those charts here. Table 1.1 is a compilation of several of the various generational charts I've seen. I'm certain you've seen something very much like this chart before. And I truly hope you don't read it; the only reason I'm putting it here is so you can be reminded of how the four-generation model is typically structured. You'll understand my subsequent arguments whether you read this chart or not. However, if you *do* choose to read it, I promise I made a few small embellishments that should entertain you.

Table 1.1 The Four-Generation Model

	Traditionalists	Baby Boomers	Generation X	Generation Y
Birth years	1900–1945	1946–1964	1965–1980	1980–2000ish
Famous people	Charlie Chaplin	Cher	Jeff Havens	Ashton Kutcher
Number of members	40 million	80 million	51 million	75–100 million
Chief influences	• Great Depression • WWII • Korean War • A bunch of other sad things	• Civil Rights • Vietnam War • Cold War • Moon landing (unless you're a conspiracy theorist)	• Dual-income families • Single parents • End of Cold War • First generation expected not to be as financially successful as their parents	• Digital media • The Internet • Portable technology
Core values	• Rule followers • Conformers • Dedication and sacrifice • Discipline • Duty before pleasure • Hard work • Loyalty • Responsibility	• Equal rights • Equal opportunities • Personal gratification • Personal growth • Spend now, worry later (or, better yet, let your kids worry about it!) • Team-oriented	• Diversity • Entrepreneurial • Independent • Informality (after all, they popularized the mullet) • Pragmatism • Self-reliance • Cynicism	• Overconfidence • Fun! • Tolerance • Social • Technologically savvy • Street smarts (despite the fact that most of them have never played outdoors)
Attributes	• Committed to employer • Financially conservative • Ethical • Organized • Strong work ethic • Task-oriented • Thrifty • Trusting	• Ambitious • Challenge authority • Competitive • Avid consumers • Live to work • Loyal to careers and employers (how this sits in the same box alongside "challenge authority" is beyond me, but there you go!) • Political correctness • Willing to take on responsibility	• Adaptable • Angry but don't know why (I like this description of us!) • Flexible • Focus on results • Free agents • Results driven • Self-starters • Strong sense of entitlement • Work to live	• Attached to their technology and parents • Multicultural • Have never lived without computers • Even more entitled than Gen Xers! • Global in their thinking • Overindulged by their Baby Boomer and Gen X parents • Innovative • Tech-dependent • Loyal to friends • Open to new ideas • Self-absorbed
Education	A dream	A birthright	A necessity	A calculated risk

	Traditionalists	**Baby Boomers**	**Generation X**	**Generation Y**
Approach to finances	• Put it away • Pay cash • Save everything	• Buy now, pay later	• Cautious • Conservative	• Earn to spend
Work ethic	• Dedicated • Pay your dues • Work hard • Company first	• Driven • Work long hours to establish identity • Quality	• Balance • Work smarter, not harder • Self-reliant • Want structure and direction	• Ambitious • Already bored with what they're doing now because they want to know what's next • Multitasking • Entrepreneurial
Technology	Adapted	Acquired	Assimilated	Integral
View on respect for authority	• Authority is based on seniority and tenure	• Started off skeptical of authority but now like it since they're in the positions of power	• Still skeptical of authority figures • Will test authority repeatedly	• Often seek authority figures when looking for guidance
View on time at work	• Punch the clock • Get the job done	• Workaholics • Invented the 50-hour work week (if, you know, you completely ignore farmers and everyone who worked in 19th-century factories, coal mines, railroads...) • Visibility is the key	• Project-oriented • Get paid to get job done	• Gone at 5 p.m. • Work is a "chore" or something that fills the time between weekends
Opinion of work/life balance	• What the hell is work/life balance?	• Worked too hard so they could buy multiple vacation homes they never have time to use. As a result, imbalance between work and family.	• Focus on clearer balance between work and family	• Flex time, job sharing, and sabbaticals
Desired work environment	• Hierarchal • Top-down management	• Democratic • Equal opportunity	• Functional • Efficient • Flexible • Informal	• Collaborative • Creative • Positive • Diverse
Think work is...	• An obligation • A long-term career	• An exciting adventure	• A difficult challenge • "Just a job"	• Like, really hard

	Traditionalists	Baby Boomers	Generation X	Generation Y
What they bring to the workplace	• Experienced • Consistent • Disciplined • Dependable • Detail-oriented • Stable	• Challenge the status quo • Good at seeing the big picture • Good team players • Mission-oriented • Go the extra mile	• Adapt well to change • Direct communicators • Determined • Good task managers • Highly educated • Multitaskers	• Consumer mentality • Great at collaboration • Fast • Optimistic
Major problems they have at work	• Don't adapt well to change • Hierarchical approach can annoy others • Typically avoid conflict • Everything is either right or wrong	• Expect everyone to be workaholics • Don't like change (anymore) • Can be pretty judgmental • Not good with finances • Self-centered	• Their cynicism can get really, *really* tedious • Dislike authority so much they sometimes ignore great ideas • Impatient • Lack people skills • Sometimes reject rules simply for the sake of rejecting them	• Distaste for menial work (or anything that doesn't look at least a little bit like a video game) • Inexperienced • Need a *lot* of supervision • Unreasonable expectations • Did I say Gen Xers were impatient? Just wait until you see *these* guys!
What you need to know to work with them	• Don't expect work to be fun • Need to know procedures • Want a disciplined working environment • Consider their feelings • They appreciate personal touches	• Need to know that their ideas matter • Because their careers define them, acknowledging the value of their work is important • Easily annoyed by unproductive routines • Need to know why their work matters, how it fits into the big picture, and what impacts it will have and on whom • Tend to like team assignments • Respond well to attention and recognition • Tend not to take criticism well	• Crave independence and informality in the workplace • Appreciate flextime so they can pursue other interests • Need to be able to have fun at work • Want the latest technology	• Want to work with bright, creative people • Want you to take time to learn about their personal goals • Want to work with friends (even when those friends are not bright or creative) • Need to know the rationale for the work you've asked them to do • Want variety • Need help navigating work/life issues • Make work personal

	Traditionalists	Baby Boomers	Generation X	Generation Y
Opinion of authority	Respectful	Impressed	Unimpressed	Indifferent
How to communicate	• One-on-one • Write a memo • Present yourself in a formal, logical manner • Show respect for their age and experience • Use good grammar • Use formal language	• "Call me anytime!" • Use a direct style of communicating • Pay attention to your body language • Answer questions thoroughly and expect them to grill you for more information • Include them in decisions • Okay to use first names • Emphasize the company's vision and mission	• "Call me only at work." • Email • Use straight talk and present facts • Learn their language and speak it • Informal communication style • Don't micromanage (like there's any group of people on the planet who LIKE being micromanaged...) • Avoid buzzwords and jargon • Connect your message to results	• "Text me." • "Or send me a picture." • "Does a phone have another function besides texting and picture sharing?" • Use positive, motivational language • Use action verbs • Be funny
Feedback and rewards	• No news is good news • Satisfaction is a job well done • Want private recognition without fanfare	• Like monetary rewards and often display all awards for public view • Like praise • Like title recognition • Want something to put on the wall	• Want to be rewarded with time off • Prefer regular feedback on their work • Need constructive feedback to be more effective (duh!) • Want structure and coaching • Like a hands-off type of supervisory style	• Need frequent feedback • Need clear goals and expectations • Need frequent communication • Want recognition • Like flex-time, work-from-home, and other creative arrangements
Messages that motivate	• "Your experience is respected."	• "You are valued." • "You are needed."	• "Do it your way." • "Forget the rules."	• "This place is fun." • "You will work with smart, creative people."

	Traditionalists	Baby Boomers	Generation X	Generation Y
How to mentor them	• Investment in long-term commitment • Show support for stability, Security, and community • Allow the employee to set the "rules of engagement" • Ask what has worked for them in the past and fit your approach to that • Respect their experience • Avoid saying they'll need to undergo radical change	• Acknowledge that they have "paid their dues" • Teach them work/life balance • Show them how you can help them • Pre-assess their comfort level with technology before new projects • Emphasize that their decision is a good one • Follow up, check in	• Offer a casual work environment • Lighten up • Be more hands-off • Listen and learn • Let them know they work *with* you, not *for* you • Appreciate that they have a life • Provide learning and development opportunities • Provide opportunities to try new things • Be prepared to answer "why" often • Present yourself as an information provider, not "The Boss"	• Encourage them to explore new avenues • Acknowledge their self-worth • Welcome and nurture them • Challenge them • Offer a custom plan specific to them • Be impressed with their decisions • Use their peers as testimonials
Attitude toward training and development	• Training should contribute to the organization's goals	• Training helps the organization but is also a path to promotion and additional compensation	• Training enhances their versatility in the marketplace • Not necessarily loyal to the company that trained them	• Willing and eager to take risks • Everything is a learning opportunity
Attitude toward retirement	• Put in 30 years, retire, and live off of pension/savings	• If I retire, who am I? • Haven't saved enough money so probably need to work at least part time	• Hope to retire early • Might want different experiences and may change careers	• Expecting to develop a killer app and retire a multimillionaire by the time they're 32 • Delusional

This is what you've heard. This is what you've seen. And it is almost completely useless.

Honestly, what manager has the time or even the *ability* to put a chart like this into practice? Who can afford to sit at a desk, putting everyone she manages or works with into this chart, analyzing their supposedly rigid attitudes about a couple dozen different elements of work, life, and the balance between them—and *then* devise solutions tailored to each person's incomprehensibly specific needs and motivations? And even if you could somehow find the time to do such an exhaustive independent analysis, the larger question remains: With so many glaring and seemingly insurmountable differences between the members of so many different generations, who can even hope to find successful managerial techniques, change management strategies, or anything else when it looks as though everyone 15 years older or younger than we are is essentially a completely different type of person?

In the interest of making it easier to describe people based on their age, we've made it enormously *more* difficult to develop real solutions for a diverse workforce.

In His Own Words: Matthew S. on Managing a Four-Generation Workforce

Matthew S. is 32 years old and works as a manager for a large financial services company. He is relatively young for a manager and works primarily with people older than he is, but most of the people he manages are younger than he. This has put him in the privileged position (if you can call it that) of being able to witness firsthand how frustrating it is to try to work with four generations at once. In his own words:

> Our company was in the process of expanding into a new metropolitan area. The person overseeing the operations, who was a Baby Boomer, spent a lot of time talking about how to set the right culture for this new operation. Those of us on the leadership team had been relocated from across the country, but the majority of the people we would be leading would be brand new to the company, and for many of them, this would be their first professional job.

> In conversations about setting the right culture, we spent weeks discussing professional dress. Our supervisor was intent on setting a professional culture and believed we could not expect excellent work if we did not dress professionally.

Many others felt the same, although some wanted to allow for relaxed standards for employees who wouldn't be customer facing. Many of the Baby Boomers and Gen Xers had grown accustomed to dressing business casual and were happy to keep it that way. Some of the oldest people on our leadership team expressed frustration that we were even having this conversation, which wouldn't have happened 20 years ago, and didn't see any need to cater to Millennial sloppiness. There was one Millennial on our leadership team, and he pointed out that it was Baby Boomers and Gen Xers who started the trend toward "dressing down" in the first place, which everyone admitted was a good point but didn't do anything to change the opinion of our supervisor. His vision of professional dress finally prevailed, and we spent many meetings trying to relay this message to other areas of the leadership team as we prepared to launch.

Then, one day, someone brought in a photo he had taken on his way into work. It was a billboard for our company, displayed prominently along a highly trafficked interstate and highlighting our arrival to the area and the career opportunities available. The woman in the picture who was to represent our "workforce" was wearing a sleeveless tank top with tattoos covering both of her arms. It was the ultimate backfire. Obviously some of the people at headquarters had been having a similar conversation to ours but had come to a different conclusion. So we were forced to reverse our plans, and our director changed his tune quickly. He went as far as to show up in jeans the next day. He later told us he'd had to go buy a pair because he hadn't owned any.

It's time for a better way. It's time to think about generational differences the way we used to before we needlessly complicated the issue and turned simple issues like how to dress for work into grueling, heated arguments between multiple factions. This book is for anyone who has grown tired of our current method of discussing generational differences. It's for anyone who has sensed that this problem may not be as difficult as we've made it out to be. And it's for anyone who thinks that we might all be a little more alike than we are different.

So say goodbye to the four-generation model because I won't be referencing it again. I might occasionally use terms like *Baby Boomer* and *Gen Xer* while making various points, but I'll only be doing so as part of the process of reframing our current four-generation model in the terms of the two-generation model we'll be discussing from here on out. If you think it arrogant or audacious to try to overturn several decades of established theory about generational differences in the workplace and replace all that with a new model, I understand why you might think so.

But to be perfectly honest, the two-generation model you're going to be reading about is not new at all. Not by a long shot.

2

The Two-Generation Model

If you've ever watched three people playing racquetball, you know how chaotic it is. Two-person racquetball is pretty straightforward: Person A hits the ball, then Person B, and then back and forth until someone scores. With three people, though, Person A is playing against Persons B *and* C—at least while serving. Then, when Person B serves, A and C team up, and later it'll be A and B against C. As you might imagine, the games are generally longer than two-person racquetball games because it's a little harder to score when you're always facing two opponents. And if you were to come in during the middle of a point, it would be fairly difficult to figure out which player had served.

This leads to an interesting observation (at least to me). While I can think of plenty of individual sports where we compete against multiple opponents—racquetball, track, and auto racing come to mind—I can't think of a single team sport that involves more than two teams competing against one another. We have individual sports where one person can defeat any number of opponents by being faster, stronger, or more skilled. We also have team sports like gymnastics where multiple teams are competing, but they're not truly competing *against* each other because they're not actively interacting; instead, each team participates separately and does not interfere in any way with the performance of the other competitors. But can you imagine how complicated football would be if there were *three* end zones? Each offense could score in two different end zones, but they'd have to get through two different defenses as well. Can you even envision a triangular basketball court? Games would end with final scores of 3–1, and players would retire at 25 because they'd all be nearly dead from exhaustion.

And do you know why we don't have these kinds of competitions? It's not because their creation is beyond us. We've made buildings that rotate in the wind, we've got 943 varieties of mustard when the world would happily have survived with merely 65, and anyone who has ever tried to make a turducken (which is a chicken stuffed into a duck and *then* stuffed into a turkey, in case you're not from Minnesota) knows that there is definitely an easier way to get all that meat shoved into your face. We could invent sports with 3 or 4 or 12 teams competing simultaneously. We could design the proper courts and stadiums, and we could figure out a system of universally acceptable rules. It would be complicated, but we could certainly do it.

But we haven't, we won't, and the reason we won't is because it isn't *natural*. In human history, we've never come up with a team sport where more than two teams at a time compete directly against one another because it has never occurred to us to do so. It's always two teams. It's the only way we know how to think about those kinds of competitions.

And...Your Point?

The point is that the current generational divisions we're operating with are similarly unnatural. It's virtually impossible not to feel overwhelmed when you feel as though you're simultaneously playing against three distinct generations. The current conversation doesn't simply complicate the issue; it actually goes against human nature.

If that sounds extreme to you, then consider that except for the seasons of the year, we divide almost nothing into fours. Our body is bilaterally symmetrical and consists of organs and sections that never occur more than twice: two eyes, two ears, two hands, two knees, two kidneys, two lungs, two nostrils, and two halves of the brain. Human beings have created hundreds of political parties over the centuries, but all of them boil down into two major categories: conservative or liberal (relative to their counterparts).[1] Returning to the sports

---

[1] And just in case you're a Green Party American or Free Democratic Party German and want to contest the nuances of our multifaceted political system, you can either vote or not vote on any given issue, and if you choose to vote, you can either vote Yes or No. Fundamentally, all of politics is the exercise of one of only two options. Yay for simplicity!

analogy, those of us who enjoy a given sport typically support only one team and reserve a special hatred for one other team more than all others. There are two biological sexes, two states of energy in the binary system that's allowing me to write this sentence,[2] two possible locations in which you might spend eternity after you die, and two types of transmissions you can choose from when you buy a new car.

Indeed, in virtually everything we do, we divide the world into twos. Men vs. Women, Republicans vs. Democrats, Axis vs. Allies (and then later East vs. West), American League vs. National League, Paper vs. Plastic, East Coast Rap vs. West Coast Rap, Ketchup vs. Mustard,[3] Pepsi vs. Coke, Introverts vs. Extroverts, Rural vs. Urban, PC vs. Mac, Nerds vs. Jocks...as you can see, we have an overwhelming tendency to divide the world into two groups. We do so because it feels natural and allows us to simplify what might otherwise be a chaotic and indecipherable mess.

Your conversation about generational issues at work shouldn't be any different. Dividing people into four generations has deprived us of the ability to provide a workable contrast against those who do things differently. By creating a situation in which every person has three supposed antagonists, current generational theory has essentially rendered all of us paralyzed, unable to know how to move forward against so many different people coming at us from so many different directions.

In fact, a simple look at today's workplace demographics is yet another reason the four-generation model is an obsolete one. First off, the so-called Traditionalists constitute around 5% of today's current workforce, which is a small enough percentage that it simply doesn't make sense to view them as a population so idiosyncratic and distinct from your other workers that they need to be coached and listened to and managed in a completely different way from everyone else. Then

---

[2] I am *so* not getting into the swamp of quantum computing, since I think it's safe to say that generational issues don't have much of a quantum component. But in case I wanted to, I would argue that in a quantum system, you know either the position or the velocity. Boom!

[3] Not quite sure why this one is such a contest since they taste totally different. But get yourself into the right online forums, and you'll soon learn that there are millions of people apparently willing to die in support of their chosen condiment.

we have approximately 75 million Baby Boomers, 35 to 40 million in Generation X, and 75 to 80 million in Generation Y. From a purely mathematical standpoint, you can easily see that two generations are dominating the workforce.

Moreover, Gen Xers tend to view themselves as a composite of the larger cohorts they're sandwiched between. They identify themselves as having some of the typical characteristics of Baby Boomers and some of the Millennials. So really, they're already trying to help simplify this picture for us by voluntarily placing themselves in one of the two larger camps.

In His Own Words: Alan S. On How Generation X Self-Identifies

Alan S. is 36 years old and thus was born at the tail end of Generation X. He recalls vividly what it was like to feel as though he belonged to two different generations at the same time. In his own words:

> I began my career working at a startup marketing firm that was predominately run by senior-level executives who had quit their jobs to start this new business. There was a good mix of ages at the company, and there were definitely times when I sided with one age group over the other. Typically I sided with the older generation when it came to behavior. When a client would come into the office, I knew how to talk to them. I was polite. I shook their hands. I looked them in the eye. I knew how to be in a business conversation, and I acted more like a Baby Boomer than a Millennial. The younger employees seemed to lack a lot of the business skill and professional etiquette techniques I assumed everyone had but obviously don't.
>
> When it came to technology and idea generation, however, I definitely identified more with my younger coworkers. I didn't relate to the experienced workers at the company. I was constantly amazed by what they were unable to do on a computer. I wondered how they ever got anything accomplished, considering that it took them four hours to figure out how to create and email a PDF.

Alan's experience is typical of many Gen Xers and, as mentioned a moment ago, provides a nice transition into the model I'm advocating in this book. To put things into a perspective we can actually work with, we need to create a functional dichotomy. That's what Alan did naturally; instead of thinking of himself as a member of a distinct generation who had nothing in common with those older or younger than himself, he identified sometimes with one group and sometimes with another.

We need to get rid of these four generations. We don't need them. To be perfectly honest, we don't even actually *use* them, at least not when we're comparing ourselves against others (more on that in a few pages). So let's replace it with something simpler and more natural. As we've already discussed, everything we do ultimately gets divided into two main opposing groups. And when you dissect the generational divide to its most fundamental level, there are really only two ways we look at one another.

There's Generation *Us*, and then there's Generation *Them*.

Generation Us and Generation Them

Throughout the entirety of human history, we've always divided the world into these two simple categories: Us and Them.[4] Us and Them is how we think about everyone and everything. We have friends and family, and everyone else is a stranger; we have people who are the same color or sexual orientation or religion as ourselves, and everyone else is not; we have people who work in our industry and people who work in other fields; we have people who work in our company, and everyone else is an outsider who can't possibly understand the issues we're dealing with or the processes that govern our business.

Because we are constantly analyzing everyone with multiple Us/Them criteria, we tend to unconsciously put everyone we meet along

---

[4] I realize that I mentioned this once in the Introduction, but I'm mentioning it here again because there's a decent chance you didn't bother to read the Introduction.

a sliding spectrum of Us and Them—a single straight line, with Us at one end and Them at the other:

US ◄──────────────────────────────────────► **THEM**

Most of us have very few people we would place all the way at the Us side of the line. Your spouse, your kids, your parents, your siblings, your closest friends—these people are probably as far on the Us side of things as anyone gets.

On the other hand, most of us have a larger (but still small) number of people who we would place all the way on the Them side: people from different countries who speak a different language, practice a different religion, eat different foods, wear different clothes (or no clothes at all), and engage in different pastimes. I'm sure you can think of some people or cultures that seem so foreign that it's hard to imagine having anything at all in common with them. Three-headed aliens that eat rocks and poop out gumballs, for instance, would probably be all the way to the right.

US ◄──────────────────────────────────────► **THEM**
(close family and friends)   (gumball-pooping aliens)

At its most basic level, this constant analysis of Us and Them governs the way we treat the people with whom we come in contact. The more we can identify Us qualities in others, the better we tend to get along; the more we identify Them qualities in others, the more we respond with hesitation, confusion, suspicion, contempt, derision, or outright hatred.

The entire history of human civilization can be viewed through this extremely simple lens. When one tribe or nation finds enough common qualities between itself and another, the two groups form trade agreements, establish military alliances, and occasionally merge into a single unified people. This is the process by which the American colonies, which did not initially function as a cohesive whole, were able to unify and oppose the British. America's original colonies disagreed on a wide variety of issues, but ultimately they chose to view one another as predominantly Us and the British as predominantly Them. The rest, of course, is history.

Similarly, when one company finds another in a similar industry with a similar vision and qualities complementary to their own, the two often begin to work together and occasionally merge. When we find someone we have a lot in common with, we become friends and sometimes marry. The history of female suffrage, civil rights, and same-sex marriage in the United States can all be explained by the slow but steady progression of a greater number of Americans viewing all three of those groups of people as more Us and less Them.

At the same time, when we realize that we no longer have very many qualities in common—when we start to see our spouses or bosses or business partners or military allies as more Them and less Us—that's when we start to separate. That's when we stop talking, get divorced, feel stifled or unappreciated at work, set up trade embargoes, and so on. I challenge you to find a single human interaction in which the constant interplay of Us and Them is not at work. It is the philosophical underpinning of absolutely everything we do. The more we see other people like Us, the better we get along. The more we see other people like Them, the more problems we have.

Your generational issues at work are functioning in exactly the same way. If you're butting heads with someone and have attributed the difficulty to generational issues, the *real* problem is that you feel as though your antagonist is more Them and less Us. When you and a same-age colleague commiserate about the chronic impatience of your young employees or lament the hopeless intransigence of the old guard, what you're really doing is identifying Us qualities in your conversation partner and Them qualities in the people you're complaining about. It's that simple.

Fortunately, this classification of Us and Them isn't a rigid or permanent one. Because each of us is constantly analyzing everyone else as Us or Them in dozens of different ways all the time, our attitudes about other people tend to shift considerably. A Christian will be friendlier toward a Muslim she works with than one who lives in a foreign country because the two coworkers have several Us qualities in common—same employer, similar job duties, possibly even similar interests—but she is likely to become *less* friendly toward a Christian friend who suddenly converts to Islam because that act moves the friend more into the Them camp. If you learn tomorrow that you and your boss share the same hobby, you'll view her in a slightly more positive light; if you learn that the two of you share 17 hobbies in common, you'll probably get along very well. If one of your friends suddenly goes on a nine-month diet comprised entirely of pickles and hummus, your relationship with that person will change in a slightly negative direction—especially if he doesn't let you give him a mint.

The goal of all this, presuming that you want to have happy and healthy relationships with the people you're forced to share the world with, is to put as many people as possible into the Us camp. And there are exactly two ways we do this (there's that number two again).

The first is to find as many commonalities as possible between ourselves and everyone else. Shared interests, shared heritage, shared goals—the more of these we find in others, the better we'll get along. To modify an earlier example, when a family with a different religion than yours ends up moving into the house next door, they're already more of an Us than they would be if they lived halfway around the world because you can easily identify specific things you have in common—similar income level, kids in the same school system, and so on.

However, finding those commonalities isn't always possible. Not everyone has the same background or education or hobbies as you, and you can't force other people to think or behave exactly the way you do. So the second way we attempt to move people into the Us camp is to try to understand *why* they act or believe the way they do because doing so allows us to put other people's behaviors and attitudes into a context we can better understand. Understanding where someone else is coming from is rarely as strong a unifier as going to the same college or being diagnosed with the same type of cancer, but it's still a powerful tool to turn Them into Us. To modify another earlier example: If you are heterosexual but see the push for same-sex marriage as a desire on the part of same-sex couples to enjoy the same kinds of relationships as heterosexual couples, you will be more likely to support them because you'll recognize an Us quality in them—namely, the desire to marry.

So far we've limited our discussion to social and cultural issues—race, religion, sexual orientation, nation-building, war, and so on. I've done this to illustrate that the Us/Them dichotomy is the defining psychological impulse behind *everything* we do. We're hard-wired to put everyone we meet into one of these two categories, and we move them closer toward fully Us or fully Them depending on a lot of different factors. The more commonalities we can find between ourselves and others and the better we can understand their motivations for doing whatever it is that they do, the more we'll view them as Us and the better we'll be able to work together. It's not a terribly complicated concept, and it works for everything. These are the only two ways that any of us ever come together.

So now that we've established a philosophical framework for solving every type of human problem (presuming, you know, that people actually want to do that), let's focus on how the Us vs. Them dynamic plays out in your professional life.

Us vs. Them, the Professional Version

Just like in our personal and cultural lives, the Us and Them dynamic plays out in every element of our professional lives as well. Management vs. employees, salaried workers vs. contractors, the people in your department vs. the people in any other department, and so on. Regardless of where you work, you will have certainly witnessed one or more of these dichotomies. All other things being equal, managers tend to align themselves more closely with other managers than with entry-level employees, and salaried workers tend to view outside consultants as more Them and less Us.

In an ideal company, everyone identifies everyone else as an *Us*. Managers, employees, customers, and shareholders all view themselves as part of a single entity with a shared and mutually beneficial goal. That's when you see a happy and productive workforce, healthy competition between departments, and all the other "we're in this together" stuff that helps companies grow and profit and make the Best Companies to Work For list and so on. If you look at the mission statement of Starbucks, for example, you'll see a dedicated effort to position everyone in their enterprise as united in purpose, from the farmers who grow their coffee to the baristas who use delicious syrups to make that coffee palatable to the shareholders who demand constant growth. Whether Starbucks is succeeding or not can be a matter of debate, but there can be no debate that their goal is to create a company where everyone is an *Us*.

In a crappy[5] company, however, workers tend to treat the people outside of their immediate circle as Them. That's when you hear employees complaining about management, customers jumping ship for a more attentive competitor, departments separating off into isolated and occasionally antagonistic silos, and so on. To use an easy example, the management at Enron treated both their customers and their employees as Them, and that attitude contributed to a self-centered culture that ultimately led to that company's collapse. More recently, the senior management at Polaroid treated digital media in general and its users in particular as something to be avoided rather than embraced—as a Them rather than Us—and in 2008 Polaroid filed for bankruptcy.

So if you're a CEO trying to figure out how to improve your company's culture, the first question you need to be asking is, "What can I be doing to create an environment where everyone is an Us?" If you're a sales manager struggling to improve relations with the people who create the products you're responsible for selling, you need to ask, "What can I do to convince our designers and developers that my goals are the same as theirs?" And if you're a new employee eager to move up in your company, you need to ask, "What can I do to persuade my managers that I'm really one of them?"

Viewing the world through an Us/Them framework, and then constantly thinking about how to move people away from Them and toward Us, is the *easiest* way to define problems and find solutions for every human issue we face—personal, professional, or otherwise.

How the Us/Them Dynamic Operates

We've discussed how the Us/Them argument plays out in the workplace in several different ways. And without question, far and away the biggest Us/Them dichotomy that we deal with in our professional lives is the cultural and intellectual divide between more-experienced workers and their less-experienced colleagues. It's a split that transcends departmental divisions and supersedes even management/staff divisions. Employees can become managers, but new

---

[5] I felt like *crappy* was a better antonym for *ideal* than *less than ideal*.

managers are almost never immediately accepted as full equals by their more senior counterparts. In the same way, workers in different departments who were hired at the same time will often find more in common with each other than they will with their younger or older colleagues in their own departments.

In fact, when we talk about generational issues in the workplace, what we're often talking about are issues of experience rather than age. We usually phrase the issue as a function of age, since *getting older* and *gaining experience* are typically synonymous. But not always.

Case in point: If you're hiring 2 entry-level account executives, or 200 entry-level call center representatives, or 2,000 entry-level computer software engineers, their age is absolutely irrelevant to the way you will train them. Whether you're talking about an 18-year-old high school graduate, a 25-year-old college graduate, a 40-year-old making a midcareer transfer from another industry, or a 52-year-old returning to the workforce after spending the last two decades raising her children, they'll all go through the same training. They'll all be given the same tools. And, most importantly, they'll all be viewed as inexperienced by your existing workforce.

That doesn't mean age isn't an issue because it absolutely is. In each of these examples, your older workforce will typically discover more Us qualities with your older hires, just as your younger staff members will connect more easily with your younger hires. The point is that age isn't the *only* factor at play here because there are some important ways in which age and experience are not always synonymous. We talk about this in more detail in later chapters, but for now it's important to note that this issue of *experience*—how we acquire it, what it teaches us, how we use it, and how it occasionally constrains and even harms our ability to innovate—is going to be a major part of our discussion.

Interestingly enough, there's almost no research to help us determine at what point a person moves from *inexperienced* to *experienced* at a given job or skill. Some studies have attempted to quantify the point at which a person becomes an expert at a given skill, and we reference those later; but there's really nothing to help explain at what point the novice transforms into the knowledgeable and respected dispenser of wisdom. For the most part, you've been left to determine that for yourself—which is something all of us instinctively do, but unfortunately we are rarely in perfect agreement with everyone else's definitions of *experienced* and *inexperienced*. What exactly constitutes "more experienced" and "less experienced" varies from industry to industry and company to company.

The "more experienced/less experienced" dichotomy is also one whose members tend not to move very quickly along the Us/Them line. If someone has 12 more years' experience as a carpenter or computer analyst or whale herder than you do, there's really nothing you can do to catch up. Until he retires or switches industries, he'll *always* have 12 more years' experience than you, and so he'll always be inclined to view you as less-experienced and therefore at least a little Them.

And if this dichotomy of age and experience isn't a perfect rule, it's absolutely true that the vast majority of us *feel* as though it is. In my capacity as a keynote speaker, I've spoken at hundreds of different events—association conferences, company meetings, leadership retreats, all-staff training days, and everything in between. Collectively I've had the opportunity to speak to representatives of several thousand different companies, everything from mother/daughter businesses to Fortune 25 companies. And whenever the subject of generational issues has come up, all of the people and companies I've spoken to—repeat, *100% of them*—have told me that their workplace *feels* as though there are a lot of workers in the more-experienced camp (however they choose to define that for themselves), a lot of workers in the less-experienced (or inexperienced) camp, and relatively few people in between to bridge that gap. This belief simultaneously reflects the hard numbers of current workplace demographics *and* reinforces the main thesis of this book that all of us instinctively want to divide things into two opposing sides for the sake of clarity and simplicity. And I'm willing to bet anything—a speedboat, a pet giraffe, whatever you want—that if I were to ask you if it *feels* as though you have a large number of highly skilled workers, a large number of new or less-skilled workers, and not enough people in between to create a smooth transition between the two, you'd say yes.

The point is, if yours is the typical workforce, then the "more experienced/less experienced" dichotomy is probably impacting every element of your business. It's a dichotomy that's both rooted in natural demographics and reinforced by our natural tendency to divide things into twos. That's why the four-generation model has to go, and that's why replacing it with a more natural two-generation approach—one that focuses specifically and relentlessly on the constant interplay between age and experience—will make the solutions to your generational issues easier than they've ever been before.

And to make things even easier (and more amusing), let's change the terms a little bit. So far I've been focusing on the terms *more experienced* and *less experienced,* but that's a little wordy and not a whole lot of fun to say. More importantly, most of the time age and experience go hand in hand. So let's call it what it really is. Every generational book you've ever read and every generational training session or keynote speech you've ever attended has danced around the truth in an effort to play nice and be polite and do all that stuff I don't really feel like doing anymore. So let's just come out with the truth.

The *real* generational issue facing your company is the endless battle between Young People and Old People.

If you're truly honest with yourself, that's how you frame generational differences at work. Your issues are unique to you and your particular situation. But whatever those issues are, you have never said to yourself, "Well, I'm a Baby Boomer with Traditionalist tendencies trying to understand the subtle nuances of Gen X and Gen Y sensibilities." You've never thought, "I'm a skeptical, self-starting Gen Xer struggling to deal with the entrenched hierarchical mentality of my Boomer superiors." Ever. In the history of ever, nobody has phrased their generation difficulties in those terms.

What you've *really* thought is:

"That punk kid doesn't have the first idea how things really work around here."

"That stodgy old windbag should just do us all a favor and retire."

These two sentences encapsulate everything you've ever thought when it comes to generational issues at work. You've had one or both of these thoughts because that's what human beings have been thinking about other human beings since we became civilized enough to get mad at each other. There are not four generations in the workplace, and there never havebeen. There are two—Young People and Old People.

In His Own Words: Alex I. on Annoying Young People

Alex I. is 48 years old and works as a factory manager for a manufacturing company. I asked him if he had any pet peeves about his new hires. He didn't need much time to give me an answer. In his own words:

They simply are not organized and have little or no sense of urgency. They have poor time management skills and unreal expectations about earnings, benefits, and future advancement. They don't understand the structure of our work and feel that they can set their hours to accommodate their needs as long as they put in their eight hours. There is a requirement on occasion to work before 8 and after 5 or even on a Saturday. It seems to surprise some new hires that we would ask them to do so, even with all the electronic tools that make it easy. They have a surprisingly difficult time adapting to the processes our company has in place. They spend too much time texting, Facebooking, tweeting, etc., and they seem to think it's perfectly acceptable for them to do that at any time, even if they're in training or a meeting or a presentation. They have a "What's in it for me?" attitude that drives me crazy, and it comes through in the questions they ask. "How much vacation and sick time do I get? Do I have to answer work-related calls after normal work hours? Can my job description be more detailed so I know exactly what I have to do and what I should give to someone else? Are company social events mandatory?" I just wish they'd focus first on doing a good job and realize that everything they want will come from that, not the other way around.

In His Own Words: Jason M. on Annoying Old People

Jason M. is 27 years old and works as a sales agent for a life insurance company. I asked him if he had any problems with the older people he works with. He needed about as much time to answer as Alex I. did. In his own words:

> Our older owners (all 65 and over) still have trouble with computers. At least once a week I get asked to help somebody with something. It's pretty basic stuff, too—how to forward an email with an attachment, how to send an email to multiple people, how to email a photo with his iPhone as soon as he takes it. One of our almost-retired owners is coasting to retirement, basically just collecting his checks and not selling anything new. He is always on his computer, which is funny because he is not really working. All he does is surf the Internet. And not good sites either. I bet last year we had to send his computer to be cleaned from viruses almost once a month. He doesn't understand that the advertisements on some sites can be bad. Now we have a new computer system and most of his sites are blocked. He came into my office the other day and asked about a site because it was blocked and complained, "We can't have fun anymore." He always forwards me perverted emails and stuff, too. It amuses me because I can see the long chain of emails between him and his friends and I don't think they know other people can see those when they forward an email.

You will not always be the Young Person or the Old Person in the conflict. I'm sure you've had issues with colleagues who are both more and less experienced than you are. I'm sure you've rolled your eyes at people who have been with your company forever, just like I'm certain you've muttered curses to yourself at people who got hired two months ago. However, whenever you butt heads with someone at work and chalk it up to a generational issue, you *always* and *automatically* position yourself as either Young or Old relative to the person you're having a problem with.

So we've finally eliminated our current, unwieldy four-generation model and replaced it with a two-generation model, Young People vs. Old People. This makes sense. Now it's time to start solving 100% of your generational issues at work. If you'll remember, that means we have to do two things: First, find as many things as possible that Young People and Old People have in common; and second, explain as well as possible why each generation thinks and behaves the way it does. The answers to both of those questions are fairly simple, and those conversations will overlap from time to time.

But before we do that, let's have a little fun.

3

Consolidating Generational Arguments (or, Let the Stereotypes Begin!)

Recall from Chapter 1 that there is no indication of anyone prior to the 1960s talking about generational differences in the workplace in the way that it's being done today. That said, problems between Young People and Old People have *always* existed. In this sense, the generational battle has been going on forever. The important point is that except for the past few decades, it's always been a two-way conversation.

Socrates has been famously quoted for his opinion about the younger generation of Greeks he was attempting to educate:

Our youth now love luxury. They have bad manners, contempt for authority; they show disrespect for their elders and love chatter in place of exercise; they no longer rise when elders enter the room; they contradict their parents, chatter before company; gobble up their food and tyrannize their teachers.[1]

As you can see, Socrates hated chattering. He also did not finesse the generations into multiple, nuanced groups. There are youth, and there are elders—end of story.

But perhaps you don't put much stock in a quote from someone who also famously said that the only thing he knew is that he didn't

---

[1] Fun fact: Even though pretty much everyone attributes this quote to Socrates (who by the way never wrote anything down), there's good reason to believe that it was written in 1907 by a doctoral student who needed an interesting ancient quotation for his thesis.

know anything. So how about this one, which is commonly attributed to a sermon delivered by Peter the Hermit in 1274:

> *The world is passing through troublous times. The young people of today think of nothing but themselves. They have no reverence for parents or old age. They are impatient of all restraint. They talk as if they knew everything, and what passes for wisdom with us is foolishness with them. As for the girls, they are forward, immodest and unladylike in speech, behavior and dress.*

Isn't it easy to imagine someone saying this today? Once again, there are two simple divisions at play—Young People and Old People.

And just so that my Younger readers don't feel unfairly maligned, here's one for you, courtesy of 17th-century French author Francois de La Rochefoucauld, whose name I'm certain I couldn't pronounce correctly:

> *Old people love to give good advice; it compensates them for their inability to set a good example.*

I could go on, but the message is clear: We've been framing the world as an Us vs. Them/Young People vs. Old People struggle for the entire history of human civilization. We've *always* used a two-genera-tion model. And it's time we start doing so in the working world.

As I mentioned in the previous chapter, you won't always be the Younger or less-experienced person, and you won't always be the Older or more-experienced person either. Throughout the rest of this book I refer to "your Older or more-experienced colleagues" and "your Younger or less-experienced colleagues," and you are given sev-eral strategies to deal with both situations because I'm certain you view your own position as a fluid and dynamic one—sometimes acting like the Older person and other times acting like the Younger.

But let's take a moment to look at where *other people* tend to place you in the two-generation world of Young People and Old Peo-ple. For some, the answer is obvious. If you're 83 years old, there's not a lot of debate. Even if 83 is the new 75, that's still older than most of the people in your office.[2]

On the other hand, it's possible you've spent more time in the 21st century than the 20th century, which means your situation is equally clear-cut. If you still aren't sure whether you're supposed to cut open the pockets on your new suit jacket, then there's no getting around the fact that you're basically still in college.

If you're somewhere in the middle, though, it might be difficult for you to know on which side of the generational divide you will most commonly find yourself. Fortunately, I've developed a 13-question quiz to help you resolve this conundrum. This quiz features in one of my keynote presentations, and you should find it both entertaining and surprisingly accurate in helping you position yourself with respect to your colleagues.

It's not a difficult quiz, and it's not something you'll have needed to study for. All of the answers will be completely intuitive, and all you'll need to keep track of is how many times you answer A or B. The answer to every question is either A or B. Because there are really only two generations, it makes sense that each quiz question would only have two possible answers.

So, are you a Young Person or an Old Person? You're about to find out![3]

The Quiz of the Ages!

1. Have you ever used a computer that required you to insert things called *disks* into a thing called a *disk drive*?

    A. Yes.

    B. I don't recognize those words.

---

[2] Also, 50 is not the new 40, and 60 is not the new 25. If you're using phrases like these, all you're really saying is that you wish you weren't as old as you are—which only makes you sound older.

[3] Seriously, take this quiz. It'll take less than 3 minutes, and it really will help. Plus it will amuse you. If you take it at lunch with some of your colleagues, it will definitely get some interesting conversations going.

2. Do you now, or have you ever, owned an 8-track tape?

   A. Yes.

   B. What the hell are you talking about?

3. When you see the words *Four Square*, what is the first thing that comes to your mind?

   A. An awesome outdoor game or maybe some wholesome barn dancing.

   B. A form of social media.

4. My typical weekend bedtime is closer to...

   A. 6 pm.

   B. 6 am.

5. Do you have any idea what a *party line* used to be?

   A. Of course I do!

   B. I'm Googling it now, but I'm guessing you're talking about cocaine?

6. In the last six months, have you sent a handwritten letter of any kind in the mail?

   A. Yes.

   B. The only thing I use handwriting for is signing checks, which by the way I don't use anymore because you can pay online for pretty much everything.

7. Do you occasionally walk from one room of your house to another, get where you were going, and then forget why you wanted to be there in the first place?

   A. Yes.

   B. No.

8. Do you ever, even occasionally, respond to the statement "How are you doing?" by complaining about the weather, your joints, or how poorly you slept last night?

   A. I'd rather not say.

   B. Who would do such a thing?

9. Do you remember when John F. Kennedy, Martin Luther King, *or* Ronald Reagan got shot?

    A. Yes.

    B. I have a vague suspicion that I should know who those people are.

10. Madonna covered "American Pie," Sheryl Crow covered "Sweet Child of Mine," and Darius Rucker covered "Wagon Wheel." How does that make you feel?

    A. They're butchering the classics and should be shot.

    B. They're breathing new life into crappy oldies.

11. Has a horse ever been your primary mode of transportation?

    A. Yes.

    B. No.

12. Which future do you think is more likely to come true?

    A. We're going to be fighting giant mutant lizards after global warming or a supervirus or nuclear war or something like that turns the world into a nightmarish wasteland.

    B. We're going to unlock the secrets of biological immortality and live in a utopia of clean energy, food materializers, teleportation, and really, *really* cool video games.

13. If you had to wait in a line for something, which of these would be a more important line for you to wait in?

    A. Food and water.

    B. The next iPhone.[4]

Congratulations! Clarity is only a few short paragraphs away.

It will come as no surprise that the A answers are the ones Old People would typically circle, while Young People would typically circle the B answers. It follows that the more A answers you have, the

---

[4] Answer honestly. This one's not A for everyone. Someone reading this right now is thinking, "Well yes, I'll concede that food and water sustain life, but what good is life without an iPhone?"

more of an Old Person you really are, while having more B answers indicates that you're more of a Young Person. You can visualize this with a simple line, divided into two segments:

As you can see, it's pretty straightforward, and there's one point worth mentioning: Although I have no way of knowing how you answered, I am absolutely certain you have some combination of As and Bs. I've presented a version of this quiz to tens of thousands of people at hundreds of corporate events across North America, and I have never yet run into anyone who has answered 13 As or 13 Bs. I suppose there are some horse-riding members of the workforce who still conduct all of their business via handwritten letters and house visits to their customer-friends, but I haven't met any, and I doubt that you work with them either. And the only people who would answer 13 Bs are either too young to be of working age or too flighty to keep a job for very long.

So I suppose our chart should really look like this:

The point of this quiz is to illustrate that the overwhelming majority of us are not generational outliers, 100% Old Person or 100% Young Person. When it comes to generational self-identification, we all fall somewhere in the middle, in exactly the same way that almost nobody would claim to be 100% conservative or 100% liberal. Old People justifiably bristle at the suggestion that their youth and vitality have finally and fully vanished, and Young People disapprove of the often condescending lack of respect the very word *young* imparts. At the same time, *young* also implies an energetic creativity that many Old People still associate with themselves, and *old* suggests a wisdom that plenty of Young People are quite confident they also possess.

So if we were to leave generational identification up to ourselves, we would all end up describing ourselves as some combination of Young Person and Old Person. That's what happens now with our current four-generation model, as many Baby Boomers demand to be respected for their technological acumen, just as plenty of Millennials contend that they work just as hard as or harder than their grandparents did. Read any op-ed piece or the comment threads on any online article about generational issues in the workplace, and you'll find a resounding chorus of people of all ages who refuse to be limited by the characteristics of their supposed "generation." Interview anyone you work with, and chances are that person will claim to have some Traditionalist qualities, some Boomer qualities, some Gen X qualities, and some Gen Y qualities. As we've said, this happens because none of us self-identifies as 100% Old Person or 100% Young Person.

However, if you work in an environment where generational tensions are at play, then you are an Old Person or a Young Person relative to the people you work with. A large cohort of your colleagues have placed you in the Them camp because of how much older or younger (or more experienced or less experienced) you are, and in order to turn Them into Us, we need to do two things: make them realize that your differing levels of age and experience aren't as divisive as they might first seem; and understand why your Older or Younger colleagues think and act the way they do.

Even in a two-generation model, it's virtually impossible to create a separation between the two that will please everybody. Just as millions of people hover on the border between Traditionalist and Boomer or Gen X and Gen Y, there are bound to be plenty of people who would dispute the logic of any age or experience level that would firmly separate Old People from Young People. In this, at least, we can all agree that we will never all agree.

But a quiz without a grading system is hardly worth taking, and the purpose of this book is to simplify the generational picture so that we can really start to solve problems. You've just taken a simple quiz, and it has a simple grading system to separate the Old People from the Young People. However, as you will see in a few pages, this separation is more symbolic than absolute.

So if you answered *A* to *7 or more questions*, you are an Old Person. Congratulations! Your AARP card should be coming in the mail sometime next week—if it hasn't arrived already. Get ready to enjoy 10% discounts on omelets and some of the best parking spaces in the country. You'd better hurry to the mall because there's a shapeless knit sweater with your name all over it. You're presumably reading this through bifocals, and it's wonderful that you think it's still important to learn things. Any day now, you'll start feeding pigeons and playing chess in the park, and you should probably get into the habit of setting an alarm every day so you don't forget when to take your pills. Don't forget to buy a plastic box to keep all your pills separate from one another! You probably know all the shortcut keys to your company's woefully outdated computer system, and because of that, you see no reason at all to update to a newer, more intuitive OS. Oh! And when you get finished reading this book, make sure you make an appointment to get your hips checked out. Chances are one of them is about to go out on you.

On the other hand, if you answered *B* to 7 *or more questions*, you are a Young Person. Way to go! Not that you had anything to do with that, of course. Any day now your baby teeth are going to fall out, and then you'll probably be getting braces. You have the patience of a gnat, or a mayfly, or a mosquito...I'm not exactly sure what the proper comparison is, but I know it's a comparison with something that dies quickly. You'll be proud to learn that you are the reason bottled water and $5 cups of coffee exist, because before you came along, those things were free! Truly, the world was a veritable utopia of free water and coffee before you convinced everyone that tap water in plastic bottles was somehow more sanitary than tap water outside of a plastic bottle. You'll pay double for anything labeled "organic," including plastic bags, and you think infographics are as rigorously researched as an actual news story. If it were possible, you'd spend your entire day staring at pictures of other people doing things. You often doubt what your friends tell you, and you're inherently skeptical of anyone claiming to be an expert on anything, but if you read it on the Internet then you immediately assume it's true. If you happen to be sitting near something sharp right now, make sure not to put it in your mouth; sharp things are dangerous! And soon, if everything goes well, you'll be moving out of your parents' basement and into a place of your very own. I'm excited for you. Paying rent feels so grown up.

And there you go: the two generations in today's workplace, decorated in all the most unflattering stereotypes we have. The Old Person mentioned above is frail, stubborn, and obsolete, while the Young Person is impatient, gullible, and dependent on others for everything.

I know you don't think of yourself as either of these caricatures. But those descriptions—or something very much like them—are *exactly* the images we automatically, ungraciously, and unfairly conjure whenever we put someone else into a different generational category than the one in which we place ourselves.

Case in point: If you are having trouble with a Younger or less-experienced colleague, then I'm certain you've had thoughts along these lines:

"Sarah is too lazy to be trusted with anything important."

"Kyle thinks that he should get a medal or something just for showing up to work every day."

"Tamika spends more time on Facebook than she does doing her job."

"Aaron can't concentrate on one thing long enough to do a good job with it."

"Kerri has no idea how our business actually works."

"None of these kids has any concept of what 'work ethic' means!"

In His Own Words: Arthur H. on What Young People Idolize

Arthur H. is 58 years old and owns a small audio-visual company. Having recently hired two new employees, he was traveling with them on their first install. In his own words:

We were talking and getting acquainted. As we were installing some high-end speakers, projectors, and other theater equipment, the conversation moved to movies. I've always enjoyed finding out what people's favorite movies are. Learning what their top 5 or top 10 are—I think it gives you some insight into who they are and what they value. I've asked this question of dozens of people, maybe hundreds, and I've come to expect some of the usual suspects to surface—*Casablanca*, *The Godfather*, *It's a Wonderful Life*, *Gone with the Wind*, maybe even *The Usual Suspects*.

But when I put this question to my two new hires, I heard a new answer, which I received with equal doses of bemusement and shock. These two young men looked at each other for a minute before coming to this consensus: "Well, it's hard to beat *Transformers*."

Arthur's story doesn't have anything to do with work, productivity, success, ambition, or any other important professional quality, at least not directly. But even here it's clear that Arthur has a bias against the tastes of his Younger colleagues and is using that to form his opinion of the people he's recently hired—and in this he is, to a greater or lesser degree, exactly like each and every one of us.

As I've mentioned before, I've spoken at hundreds of corporate events in almost every industry there is. I've had long conversations with thousands of older and very experienced workers from every kind of background—rural and urban, blue collar and white collar, Republican and Democrat and every shade in between—and time and time again, they complain about the same things. Today's Young People are lazy, unmotivated, entitled, more interested in Facebook than productivity, and they have absolutely no sense of loyalty.[5]

On the other hand, if you're Younger than many of your colleagues and have ever had trouble with someone Older or more experienced than you are, then you've thought something along these lines:

"Barry has no idea how things really work anymore."

"Laura only wants to do it that way because it's what she's always done. She won't even listen to another approach!"

"Maurice just doesn't realize that we can't keep doing business the way he did it in 1992!"

---

[5] They never say "Today's Gen Xers" or "Today's Millennials," by the way. They say, "Today's young people." That's one of the many reasons I decided to write this book.

"Sofia's retired in all but name. She's completely checked out, totally unreliable."

In Her Own Words: Joan L. on the Example Her Older Colleagues Are Setting

Joan L. is 29 years old and works as an adjunct professor at a small private university. She'd been in her new position for less than a month when the following happened. In her own words:

> The professor across the hall from me actually took naps in his office with the door wide open. I would have people in my office, and our conversations were disrupted by the loud snores coming from across the hall. I wish I were kidding. He was tenured, which meant he basically couldn't get fired and knew it. It sets a terrible example, and it's enormously frustrating as there are fewer and fewer tenured positions every year, and he's occupying a privileged position that anyone else would make better use of than he is.

If you can identify with Arthur, Joan, or both of them, then you'll know that you've really been operating with a two-generation model all along. Our brains instinctively divide everything into Us/Them categories, and now you should be able to see that your generational issues at work are no different.

Two Visions of the Future

Now you know which generation you belong to, as well as some of the attitudes others have about your kind of people. So let's take the stereotypes a step farther.

You're about to read how the future might look if it were run *entirely* by people significantly Younger or less experienced than you are. What you're about to read may scare you. You may even cry a little. But you'll also agree that this hyperbolized version of the future echoes some of the unkinder thoughts you have had about the Youngest members of today's workforce.

What the World Would Look Like if Young People Ran Everything

The workday begins at 10:30 am. Or maybe at noon, or maybe tomorrow. The point is that it definitely starts after everyone has spent a vigorous morning playing video games and hanging out at a coffee shop discussing music no one else has ever heard of. Regardless of the industry, people show up to work wearing sweatpants, or parkas with sandals, or whatever they grabbed off the floor as they were running out the door. It isn't uncommon to see thong straps gracing the exposed midriffs of executive vice presidents and purple dreadlocks become *de rigueur*. Everyone brings their dogs to work, and those dogs poop everywhere. All business is conducted via text, and eventually all company prospectus reports look like this:

> 3Q26 Rprt re Biz Rngs
>
> Biz is gr8! Shrs r ↑12%! OMG!
>
> R cmptitrs r ↓avg 19%. LMAO!
>
> We b #3 re mkt shr by 2Q27. Swt!
>
> GTG, BB n 3 mos!
>
> BFFs!
>
> Mgmt.

The "work from home" movement swiftly gives way to the "pretend to work from home" movement, which is in turn supplanted by the "why pretend? I just really don't feel like working today" movement. Everyone gets promoted every three weeks because promotions are a great way to boost self-esteem, and companies collapse under the direction of 643 CEOs. Sick days are replaced with "sad days," "tired days," and "feeling-a-little-overwhelmed-today" days.

Standard office furniture is replaced by medicine balls and jungle gyms and treadmills on which you can theoretically walk and work but that end up just being for walking. What few things actually do get accomplished only happen between 11 a.m. and 1:30 p.m., and most of that is taken up with lunch. Naptimes become institutionalized, and pick-up games of kickball pepper the halls of every company worth working for.

As a result of this overemphasis on caprice and personal happiness, most of the functions that we currently associate with modern business disappear. Customer service is one of the first things to go, since it requires actual phone calls or (horror of horrors!) face-to-face interaction. At some point it is decided that any industry that can't be turned into an app and downloaded onto an iPad is not important enough to maintain. Privacy also completely disappears, and eventually the fact that there was ever a conversation about privacy rights is lost to history. Eventually everyone gets cameras implanted into their eyeballs so they can constantly record everything they see everywhere they go. Nobody worries about the implications of that, though, because the government probably won't ever do anything bad with all that surveillance, and anyway nobody's read *1984* because it's, like, really long.

Presidential elections are changed to occur every 43 days, and the winner is determined by whoever can get the most Twitter followers. Once Justin Bieber wins, he changes the national anthem to "If I Wuz UR President," which causes everyone over 40 to die instantly from massive (and not entirely unpleasant, given the circumstances) heart attacks. Senate votes feature the authors of various bills doing wicked-cool YouTube videos to promote their causes, and the ideas that go viral are the ones that become law. The number of bills related to funny things that cats do skyrockets, and the flag is changed to feature the really cute baby from that video all your friends forwarded you last week. While these reforms dominate the national conversation, services like road building and wastewater management and crop subsidies and disaster insurance and educational initiatives and retirement planning all vanish because thinking about those things is boring.

By 2031, human beings are extinct.

Is this a fair version of the way today's Young People really operate? Of course not. But it *is* a realistic exaggeration of the way that Young People are often portrayed—lazy, entitled, undisciplined, disinterested in working hard, captivated by whatever's newest regardless of its ultimate utility, and everything else we discussed earlier in this chapter. This vision, or something very much like it, represents our worst thoughts about the people we work with who are Younger or less experienced than we are.

Now let's look at the world we might inherit if everyone Older than you were given total control over every idea and decision.

What the World Would Look Like if Old People Ran Everything

The workday begins promptly at 8:00 a.m. It also ends promptly at 4:30 p.m. because everyone everywhere is required to be productive during exactly the same hours. People are allowed 30 minutes for lunch—23 minutes to eat and 7 minutes to travel to and from the cafeteria, where all of the food is soup. It is considered generous when cafeterias offer several different kinds of soup, and on special days there are also low-sodium rice cakes, chosen specifically because putting sodium into rice cakes is a little too crazy, and besides everyone has high blood pressure. Everything everywhere tastes like fiber, and new hires are given standard-issue orthopedic insoles as part of their orientation package.

People accept mandatory unpaid overtime as the duty of the diligent worker, and it is common to overhear conversations about "the good of the company" conducted with the same militant zeal that Cold War communists used to talk about "the good of the Party." Eventually the phrase, "That's not how we've always done things" is written into the Constitution, which inspires countries around the world to similarly amend their own charters. The push to honor tradition continually gains more and more traction, and eventually disputes are settled by swordfight. People pose for pictures for 18 minutes while they wait for the gunpowder to ignite on that silvery flash plate thing they used to use in old photographs, and eventually everyone forgets how to smile.

Somewhere along the line it's determined that 1972 is the year after which nothing new should have been invented, and so there is a huge push to return the world to a simpler state of being. Innovation ceases entirely. Buildings everywhere are designed to look like they did in the 1970s, which means that every city in the world has all the aesthetic grandeur of a sturdy, endless prison. People come to work wearing plaid leisure suits and carrying carpeted briefcases. Wheels on luggage are made illegal, and people everywhere get really strong shoulders and forearms from hauling their baggage on and off of airplanes, where smoking is once again encouraged. Flat-screen TVs are taxed at exorbitant rates, and families spend a couple Saturdays rearranging their living rooms to figure out how to fit a giant cathode-ray TV back in them. Not that there's much reason to do so, because it should go without saying that late-night television is ridiculously boring.

I'm not sure that people would end up going extinct in this version of the future, but I think we can all agree that there'd really be no reason for us to go on living.

Again, this is hardly a fair assessment of your Older or more-experienced colleagues. But once again, it's a hyperbole rooted in the biases and prejudices that many of us have about those people—namely, that they are rigid, inflexible, slow to adapt, and enslaved to protocol even in instances where that protocol doesn't work very well.

As I've said several times already, the point of this book is to simplify the question of generational differences in the workplace and put things into a framework where solutions come easily and intuitively, and these two caricatures are actually helpful. Because if you'll notice, and if you'll reflect upon your own attitudes toward the generational tensions you've experienced in your life, the differences between Younger and Older workers that we've been discussing (and exaggerating) over the past few chapters can be distilled into four major points of contention:

1. **Loyalty and work ethic**—Older workers think Younger workers have a poor work ethic and little if any sense of loyalty, while Younger workers think their Older colleagues are reluctant (or flat-out refuse) to give them any credit for the work they do.

2. **Career advancement**—Older workers think many of their Younger counterparts have unreasonable expectations when it comes to how quickly they'll move forward in their careers, while Younger workers think many Older workers have become

too complacent and stagnant in the positions they've held for the past several years.

3. **Innovation**—Younger workers think their Older colleagues are too married to outdated practices, while Older workers think their Younger counterparts have too little respect for established processes and strategies.

4. **Approach to change**—Older workers think Younger workers are too capricious and value change for change's sake, while Younger workers think Older ones are too rigid and fear any change they did not think of on their own.

These four core concepts encompass 99% of the generational issues you will face in the workplace. They're the same issues embodied in the quotes at the beginning of this chapter. Peter the Hermit is complaining that Young People are lazy, irreverent, and contemptuous of the traditions and wisdom of their elders; and Francois de La Rochefoucauld is denigrating Old People for persisting in a comfortable but outdated course of action that hasn't worked very well.

Also, these four points of contention have nothing at all to do with Gen Xers being inherently skeptical of authority, Traditionalist workers being universally enamored of rigid hierarchies, or any of the other qualities that are commonly attributed to one "generation" only. In every instance, these points of contention are a function of the ways we all change as we age and gain experience, combined with the effect of our recent technological revolution and how it has affected in different ways the people who came of age before or after its advent.

Hopefully you can now see how simple your generational issues really are. Instead of the endless confusion you saw in the chart in Chapter 1 (which I *still* hope you didn't read, unless you were having trouble sleeping one night, in which case knock yourself out), you've now distilled the generational issues separating you from your colleagues into a collection of concepts you can count on one hand.

The next four chapters are going to tackle each of these issues in turn—first loyalty and its effect on work ethic, then career advancement, then the tension between stasis and innovation, and finally the adoption or rejection of specific changes. Each chapter does two things:

- Illustrate what Young People and Old People have in common with respect to loyalty, work ethic, career advancement, innovation, and change (which will help move everyone closer to the Us side of the Us/Them line).

- Explain why Young People and Old People sometimes think differently about loyalty, work ethic, career advancement, innovation, and change (which will provide you with the strategies you'll need to successfully manage anyone who approaches these issues differently than you do).

By the end of the next four chapters, you will have all the knowledge and strategies you'll need to make your generational issues a thing of the past.

So why is it that all the Young People you work with are so evil and broken? And why are all your Old People colleagues so boring and inflexible? You're about to find out.

Core Causes of Generational Tensions in the Workplace

1. **Loyalty and work ethic**—Older workers think Younger workers have a poor work ethic and little if any sense of loyalty, while Younger workers think their Older colleagues are reluctant (or flat-out refuse) to give them any credit for the work they do.

2. **Career advancement**—Older workers think many of their Younger counterparts have unreasonable expectations when it comes to how quickly they'll move forward in their careers, while Younger workers think many Older ones have become too complacent and stagnant in the positions they've held for the past several years.

3. **Innovation**—Younger workers think their Older colleagues are too married to outdated practices, while Older workers think their Younger counterparts have too little respect for established processes and strategies.

4. **Approach to change**—Older workers think Younger workers are too capricious and value change for change's sake, while Younger people think Older ones are too rigid and fear any change they did not think of on their own.

Part Two
Solving the Problem

4

On the Nature of Loyalty and Its Effect on Work Ethic

By now you've seen a lot of statistics that all say the same thing: Workplace loyalty is dead or dying. A 2011 Careerbuilder.com study found that 76% of full-time workers would leave their current workplace immediately if the right opportunity presented itself. A 2012 MetLife survey of employee benefits, trends, and attitudes revealed that workplace loyalty is at a seven-year low, with one out of every *three* employees saying they plan to leave their jobs by the end of the year. And a 2012 Ernst & Young survey found 69% of respondents believe that employees will be even less loyal to their organizations in five years than they are today. There are plenty more, but let's stop because I'm starting to depress myself.

The loss of workplace loyalty is typically attributed to the massive influx of Young workers, whose capricious job-hopping is a reflection of their general indecisiveness and specific disinterest in working as hard as their older colleagues. That opinion is so firmly ingrained in Older workers, in fact, that a 2014 survey of 6,000 Young workers and HR professionals found that while over 80% of Young workers (ages 18–26) believed themselves to be loyal to their employers, only *1%* of human resource professionals believed the same about the Young workers they employed.[1]

---

[1] As further proof that loyalty and work ethic are inextricably linked, the same survey found that while 86% of Young workers think themselves to be hard working, only 11% of their Older colleagues thought the same.

In Her Own Words: Ellen H. on How Loyalty Has Changed

Ellen H. is 51 years old and works as a senior-level executive for a global manufacturing company. She has been with her company for over 20 years and has overseen factory operations on four continents. When I asked her how employee loyalty has changed during her career, here's what she had to say:

> Loyalty has changed significantly since I started working for my company. Back then we looked for a career, someplace we could grow and develop with an employer who would develop and grow us. My company sponsored fantastic training programs to develop future organizational leaders, three-year-long rotations in various areas requiring physical moves which cost the company anywhere from 30K to 100K. If you were in one of these programs you knew that you were being groomed for leadership. Twenty years ago, turnover was almost non-existent.

> Today, however, we see young managers enter the program to be trained by senior leaders like myself. They're given preference in job placement at the end of the rotation; they're offered a promotion—and many of them bolt the company at the first offer of 5% more in income from one of our competitors. It's enormously frustrating to spend several years and hundreds of thousands of dollars training someone only to have them abandon us the first chance they get. That never used to happen, literally never.

Obviously, the disconnect between Young People and Old People on the subject of loyalty and work ethic is a significant one. It's almost certainly a disconnect you've faced yourself. But as you're about to see, the notion that today's Young People aren't as loyal as they used to be isn't quite as true as most people think. More importantly, you're also about to find out that whenever workplace loyalty is absent, there are often some very good reasons to explain its absence.

The Importance of Loyalty

The expectation of loyalty is a fundamental quality of every kind of human relationship. If you have children, you expect them to listen to your ideas and advice more than they do to those of other adults. If you have a spouse, you expect him or her to be faithful. If you have friends, you expect them to invite you over and occasionally help you move for nothing more than a few pieces of pizza. If you have employees, you expect them to follow your rules and serve as advocates to potential customers for whatever products and services you offer. In all of these cases, you expect these people to treat you with a certain level of respect.

In fact, loyalty may be *the* defining element of what actually constitutes a functional relationship. Consider all of the healthy relationships you have with everyone you know—spouse, parents, children, friends, colleagues, bosses, employees, community members, and anyone else you interact with on a regular basis. You probably don't love all of those people, nor do you benefit financially from all of them. However, in *every* significant relationship you have, loyalty is a foundational component. To greater or lesser degrees, you expect all these people to listen when you speak, to value your contributions, and to support you when support is necessary. Therefore, when loyalty is present, a healthy relationship is possible. When loyalty is not present, a healthy relationship cannot exist.

Philosophical discussions aside, there is absolutely no disputing the value a company enjoys by having a loyal workforce. It's almost axiomatic that loyal workforces are more productive, experience less turnover, and produce more innovation than their disloyal counterparts. Here we can see the strong connection between loyalty and work ethic, a connection that is reinforced in the HR study mentioned earlier. Loyal people work harder—it's as simple as that. Or, to put it into other terms, loyalty brings everyone closer to Us, and the lack of it makes everyone just as strongly Them.

But how are you supposed to foster loyalty when today's Young People flat-out refuse to be loyal to anything but themselves? And why are they so stubbornly disloyal in the first place? Can an entire generation of people truly be that lazy and self-absorbed?

Could be. Anything's possible. To figure it out, let's take a closer look at the loyalty of today's Young People.

Are Today's Younger Workers Really Less Loyal Than Previous Generations?

According to the Bureau of Labor Statistics, the average tenure of workers aged 55–64 in 2010 was 10.3 years. That's more than three times greater than the 3.2-year average tenure of workers aged 25–34 years. Moreover, a 2013 Labor Department survey found that today's Young People have worked an average of 6.3 jobs between the ages of 18 and 25. These statistics have often been used to criticize Young People for lacking both a healthy work ethic and any sense of loyalty to their employers.

So case closed, right? Today's Young People simply aren't loyal to anyone but themselves.

Wrong. These numbers don't come anywhere close to telling the whole story.

First off, it makes absolutely no sense to compare the average tenure of today's 25- to 34-year-olds with today's 55- to 64-year-olds because our average tenure tends to increase as we get older. Most of us spend the beginning of our professional lives experimenting with a few different jobs—or falling victim to the occasional wave of "last hired, first fired"—before finding a promising opportunity and settling into a stable career. In fact, it's impossible for a 25-year-old to have worked with the same company for 10.3 years since (news flash coming): They would have needed to start working at 15, and most of the jobs we're able to do at 15 aren't the same jobs we'd like to be doing when we're 47. I was detassling corn when I was 15, and nobody wants to be doing that job for 10.3 years.

Instead, it makes far more sense for us to compare various age groups with their same-age peers from different time periods. If today's Young People are indeed less loyal than they used to be, then we should expect to see a historical decrease in the average tenure of 25- to 34-year-olds. The Monthly Labor Review and Bureau of Labor Statistics have done us the favor of keeping track of these numbers for four age groups (25–34, 35–44, 45–54, and 55–64) since 1951. Figure 4.1 shows what they've found for men, and Figure 4.2 shows the graph for women.

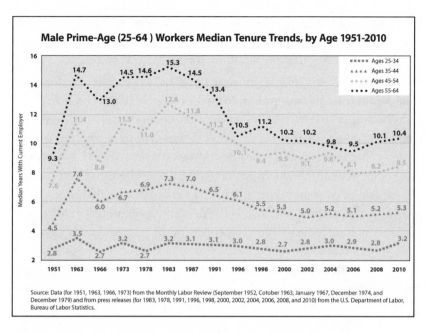

Figure 4.1 Historical trends in workplace tenure for men, 1951–2010.

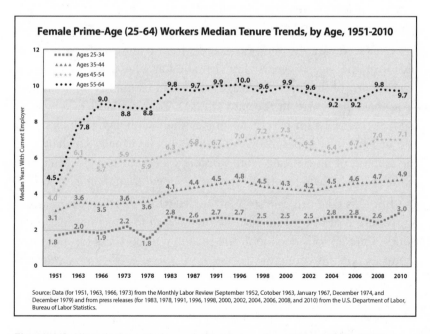

Figure 4.2 Historical trends in workplace tenure for women, 1951–2010.

As you can see, our earlier hypothesis is correct: The older we get, the more loyal we become. This has been true for men and women in every age group, without exception, for the past 65 years.

You'll also notice a significant spike in average tenure for men and women in all age groups in two places: between 1951 to 1963 and between 1978 to 1983. The first reconciles nicely with our collective memory of the 1950s being a paradise of workplace loyalty and a return to normalcy after the chaos of World War II, a nostalgic view that actually seems to be validated here. The other can be easily explained by remembering what happened during that time—specifically, the recession of 1980–1982, which saw interest rates above 21%. Apparently recessions cause people of all ages to stay at their jobs longer than they might have before, perhaps because of a lack of acceptable alternatives. The same thing seems to be happening today, as you'll notice an increase in average tenure for all age groups and both sexes from 2006 to 2010, which coincides nicely with the recent recession of 2007 to 2009.[2]

These charts show that loyalty tends to increase with age and that recessions tends to result in an increase in worker loyalty (although maybe not for the reasons most employers would prefer). Now let's address the supposed disloyalty of today's Young workers.

Let's start with the men. Look at the tenure line for 25- to 34-year-olds over the past 65 years. It's virtually flat—far more so than the lines for any of the older three age groups. In fact, far from being less loyal than they were in the past, today's Young male workers have been at their jobs for exactly as long as their same-age peers in 1973 and in 1983. In the past 40 years, there's been virtually no change in the amount of time young male workers spend at their jobs. In other words, today's Young workers are *not less loyal than they used to be.*

But let's take this one step farther. Starting in 1983, where average tenure is at or near an all-time high for all four age groups, you'll notice a precipitous decline in the subsequent 30 years for every age group *except* the youngest. To be more specific, 35- to 44-year-old

---

[2] Also, all male age groups and all but the oldest group of female workers experienced a spike in average tenure between 1966 and 1973, during which time the Arab oil embargo caused a serious recession.

men are 27% less loyal than they were in 1983; 45- to 54-year-olds are 34% less loyal; and 55- to 64-year-olds are 32% less loyal. You can argue that outsourcing, layoffs, early retirement, and corporate restructuring have all played parts—and we discuss those arguments shortly—but the fact remains that workers between the ages of 35 and 64 are staying at their companies for less time than they used to, while the rates for the youngest workers have remained constant.

The results for women are quite different. Across all age ranges, their average tenure has climbed steadily, and with few interruptions, for the past 60 years. Naturally, this is a result of women entering the workforce in greater numbers and into more professions over the past several decades. In their case, Older female workers haven't experienced the same drop in tenure since 1983 as their male counterparts. We discuss reasons for the difference between the trends in male and female tenure rates a bit later in this chapter. But with respect to the relative loyalty of Young People, it's telling that young female workers are more loyal than they have ever been. Indeed, 2010 is the high-water mark for women in the workplace, at least as far as tenure is concerned.

The numbers don't lie. Today's Young People are as loyal or *more* loyal to their employers than at any time since 1966. You could argue that the recent recession has had something to do with it, but because that recession has affected people at every age level, it doesn't seem a particularly relevant argument. You could argue the validity of these statistics, but the Bureau of Labor Statistics is hardly a biased source. Or you could concede that the Youngest members of today's workforce are actually more loyal than anyone wants to give them credit for.

Oh, and you remember the seemingly outrageous 6.3 jobs that today's Young People have before their 25th birthday? Well it turns out that the average Baby Boomer had 5.5 jobs before his or her 25th birthday. In fact, the typical Baby Boomer held 11 jobs between the ages of 18 and 44, which translates to a new job every 2.5 years.

In His Own Words: R. Li on the Career Arc of a Baby Boomer

R. Li is 67 years old and recently retired from the insurance industry. However, that isn't where he started his career, not by a long shot. In his own words:

By the age of 45, I had worked in 10 different jobs and had lived in 6 states. I was born and raised in Georgia, where I left junior college at 19 to enter the military as a medic. After my enlistment ended, I took a job selling mobile homes for a few months. That led to selling inexpensive insurance, where I collected the weekly payments door-to-door from my customers. Then I resumed my college career, majoring in writing for the film industry. After college I worked in public relations for the Boy Scouts of America for 1 year, followed by 3 years in life insurance sales in Atlanta. After that I headed to Tulsa, where I worked as a professional recruiter of computer professionals for 3 years. While in Tulsa, I also founded an oil and gas exploration company, as well as an asphalt paving company, which isn't as far-fetched as it might seem since petroleum is a major component of asphalt. Life then took me back to Georgia, where I once again put my college degree to good use by working as a writer and editor in the newspaper business for 6 years. Only after all of that did I begin my final career in property and casualty insurance, which took me to Florida, Colorado, and Illinois, where I eventually retired after 15 years.

I wouldn't call my career path a normal one, but there are plenty of my peers who have followed similarly winding roads—so many, in fact, that I'm not exactly sure what a "normal" career path really is. Perhaps it was restlessness on our part, or maybe adventure. Whatever the reasons, my sometimes tumultuous life led me into new and different experiences that never failed to stretch my abilities and my endurance. With each new endeavor, I encountered challenges that constantly prevented me from ever entering a so-called comfort zone. I was constantly learning and growing, right up until my retirement.

R. Li's story is a vivid example of an easily forgotten truth: For at least the past 60 years (and probably much longer than that), a certain percentage of Young People have been experimenting with several jobs before finally settling into a stable career. This is not a recent phenomenon. In roughly the same numbers, today's Young People are behaving exactly the way today's Old People did when they were Young People.

More importantly, today's Young People are quantifiably *more* loyal than at any other point in the past 50 years. The opinion that most Older or more-experienced workers have about Young People being more capricious and disloyal than ever is simply *not true*.

How Is This Possible?

There are several reasons to explain why today's Young People are more loyal than ever. As we've already mentioned, recessions tend to have a positive impact on worker loyalty at all age levels. When there aren't as many jobs to go around, people are often happy simply to have a job to go to—and even if they're not happy, it's not like they can do much about it.

Another significant factor is the wealth of resources that today's Young People can employ in the search for the right job. Their ability to comprehensively research prospective employers, coupled with the educational world's increased emphasis on doing so, has made it easier for people of all ages to search for jobs that fit their particular skills and interests. Although this occasionally means that Young People delay entering the working world in the hopes of finding the "perfect" job, it also means they are more likely to stay at whatever job they find because they already know ahead of time that it's probably a good fit.

But perhaps most importantly, today's Young People crave permanence in their lives—probably more than at any other time since the 1950s. As we've already discussed, the average Baby Boomer held 11 jobs between the ages of 18 and 44, which provides an interesting counterpoint to a 2013 Ernst & Young study that revealed a full 60% of the Youngest members of today's workforce expect to work for fewer than 6 employers. Young People are also the *least* likely age group to view starting their own company as the most attractive employment option, given that doing so is often a risky, uncertain, and lonely enterprise.

There's only one way to interpret data showing that today's Young People expect to work for fewer employees than their elders and that they are also comparatively disinterested at going out on their own. They simply want to be loyal to someone, *and they're actively looking for it*.

So what do today's Young People have in common with the workforce of the 1950s? The comparison is stronger than you might first think. Following the chaos of World War II, the collective desire to return to a normal, stable life was a powerful factor in helping create the golden age of work ethic and loyalty for which the 1950s are remembered. In the past 30 years, there has been a similarly world-altering phenomenon, albeit completely different in nature. And while it has affected all of us, its impact on Young People's desire for connection and permanence has been greater and more profound.

I'm talking, of course, about the Internet and how it has forever changed the way we interact with and find our place in the world. The vast majority of Gen Xers (myself included) and all Baby Boomers were born before the Internet truly took off, which means we developed our sense of self in a fundamentally different world than our younger colleagues have done. The importance of that fact cannot be overstated. If you have ever struggled to understand why your Young counterparts behave the way they do, appreciating the impact of the Internet is essential.

But before we get to that, we first need to discuss a little concept called Dunbar's number.

What Is Dunbar's Number, and Why Should I Care?

In the early 1990s, an Oxford University anthropologist named Robin Dunbar published his findings on the limits of human social interaction. Specifically, he had set out to learn whether there is a neurological limit to the number of people any one person can actively care about. In other words, he wanted to determine how many friends, family, colleagues, and neighbors you can honestly, truly consider to be part of your social sphere.

I'll spare you the research details, considering they involve regression analyses and confidence intervals and other statistical math that might put you to sleep, but the results were pretty clear: Human beings do seem to have an upper limit on social connections the brain is designed to accommodate, and that number is roughly 150. The actual range is probably somewhere between 100 and 230, and other researchers have argued that the maximum is somewhere around 300. However, 150 has become known as *Dunbar's number*. Dunbar's number is a scientific approximation of the number of people we're able to care about at any given time, and in that sense it's very similar to the 10,000-hour approximation that Malcolm Gladwell popularized in his book *Outliers* as the number of hours of practice you need in order to become an expert at something.

Dunbar's estimated maximum of 150 social connections has been corroborated in a number of different and intriguing ways. The average Neolithic farming village is estimated to have had a population of around 150 people, as did the average 18th-century English village. The basic unit of ancient Roman armies? 150, which is remarkably close to the size of the modern American military company of 160. Perhaps more impressively, in 2010 Dunbar conducted a study with Facebook to analyze user habits and found that regardless of the actual size of a person's friend network—including those with thousands of connections—the average user doesn't interact with more than 150 of those people. Even less scientific facts such as the tendency of weddings to have 300 guests or fewer (150 each for the bride and groom) support the theory that we have a built-in mental limit to the number of social connections we can pay attention to at any given time.

The reason Dunbar's number is important is because it addresses human connection, and loyalty is about nothing if not our connection to others. All of us want to belong to something, both personally and professionally, and it seems as though we're generally looking for no more than 150 people with whom to connect. There are certainly some people who have more than 150 close connections, just as some people have fewer. But I'm comfortable assuming that when you think about the number of people you consider to be important to you in some way, it's probably not more than a couple hundred.

Now, let's look at how the Internet has changed the way we go about finding those connections—and, more importantly, why it's possible to say with complete certainty that Young People are actively seeking a connection with you and your organization.

The Rise of the Internet and Its Effect on the Desire for Loyalty

It is impossible to overstate the impact of the Internet on the world today, so I'm not going to bother going into any detail. You already know the Internet is a big deal. I would even go so far as to say that it's a bigger deal than sliced bread, since—let's be honest—bread is amazing, but it didn't take a genius to figure out that you needed to cut it in order to fit it into your face. But what does the Internet have to do with the desire of today's Young People for loyalty?

In a word, everything.

I'm 36 years old as I'm writing this, which is as good an age as any to use as a dividing line between the two groups into which the Internet has split the world—people who came to maturity *before* the Internet truly took hold and people who came to maturity *after* the Internet became inextricably entrenched in our daily lives. This division, by the way, is a part of the reason that we Gen Xers are often characterized as being perpetual outsiders. Many of us honestly don't know where we fit because we straddled this technological revolution.

And it was undeniably a revolution.

If you came of age in the world before the Internet, then you grew up in a world without constant connections. You played outside far more than kids do today because there was a good chance you didn't own a video game system, and you ran or rode your bicycle to your friends' houses to see if they were home because most of the time it was actually quicker than trying to get them on the phone.

In fact, let's look at just how small the world of yesteryear really was.

The World Old People (Myself Included) Grew Up In

- People answered the phone by saying, "Hello?" like it was a question because it was. You didn't know who was calling. It could be a friend, it could be a telemarketer, or it could be the police—you just didn't know!

- The original "mobile phone" was the phone in your house that had the longest cord. That phone was usually in the kitchen, and that cord was just shy of a mile long. It allowed you to talk on the phone in up to *two rooms*!

- People memorized other people's phone numbers because there was no other choice. Also, when you made plans to meet with your friends in a public location, you would arrive at the agreed-upon destination and then...wait for it...waaaait for it... you'd just walk around until you found each other. Nobody had geolocation software on their phones, mostly because nobody had phones in their pockets and the word *geolocation* hadn't actually been invented. How did anyone ever find anyone? It's still a mystery.

- Somewhere in the 1980s, camcorders became available. They weren't exactly popular, but it wasn't uncommon to see parents everywhere with a suitcase-sized camera perched precariously on their shoulders. Nobody ever learned how to remove the time stamp from anything, and it was about 15 years before a more compact device came along. Also—and this is important for later—nobody ever saw your home movies unless they were physically in the presence of the VHS tape that it was stored on. The number of home videos that went viral was exactly zero.

- In 1950, there were 12 television channels available, a number that barely changed for the next 35 years. In 1961 FCC chairman Newton Minow describes the vast majority of television as a "procession of game shows, violence, audience participation shows, formula comedies about totally unbelievable families, blood and thunder, mayhem, violence, sadism, murder, Western badmen, Western goodmen, private eyes, gangsters, more violence, and cartoons, and, endlessly, commercials, many screaming, cajoling, and offending, and, most of all, boredom"—which just goes to show that people's opinion of television has been the same since pretty much forever. The number of options for being bored, however, really started to take off around 1985. In that year the average home had 18 television channels; in 1990 it was 33; by 2000 the number had swelled to 61; and by 2014 the average American home would have 189 available channels.

- On March 13, 1984, the first handheld cellphone was sold. The Motorola DynaTAC 8000X was 13 inches long and 3.5 inches wide, weighed 28 ounces, had enough battery life for a 30-minute phone call, and cost $3,995. It took 6 years for a pocket-sized version to be developed, which carried a 75-minute battery life and a more modest $2,995 price tag. As you can imagine, almost nobody owned one. It was 10 *more* years until the first Internet-equipped cell phone became available in 1999.

- Speaking of the Internet, it first debuted to the public in 1991, but it was four years before the first search engine (Yahoo!) made it possible to find anything. That helps explain why, in 1995, only 18 million American homes had modems, and 32% of those people said they wouldn't miss the Internet very much if it were to disappear. In fact, only 20% of Internet users in 1995 went online every day. To quote a hilarious article from 1995, "Few see online activities as essential to them, and no single online feature, with the exception of E-Mail, is used with any regularity. Consumers have yet to begin purchasing goods and services online, and there is little indication that online news features are changing traditional news consumption patterns." By 2000 the number of online users in the United States had exploded to 132.2 million, but that was still only 47% of the country.

- Oh, and did I forget to mention that virtually the *only* kind of Internet connection that existed during the 1990s was dial-up? That means that for a full decade, everyone who used the Internet had this conversation with their family members: "Don't pick up the phone, please! I'm just going to check my e-mail;[3] I'm pretty sure I have one or two of them. Should only take

---

[3] Which I intentionally wrote with a hyphen because we hadn't eliminated that yet.

18 minutes for them to load, unless they attached a picture, in which case I'll have to stare at my screen for a solid hour while the image loads line by line. So just DON'T PICK UP THE PHONE!!!!"

As you can see, if you grew up before the Internet really took off, there were several years—occasionally decades—between the advent and widespread adoption of these various pieces of technological connection with our friends, family, and the rest of the planet. Also, each of these innovations was originally dedicated to a single and specific type of communication: cell phones for calling, video cameras for recording, and computers for email and other written pieces. It took the better part of 20 years for the Internet to allow for the easy transfer of images across data lines, for cell phones to allow for written text messages, and for video cameras to be packaged into desktop computers and later smartphones. Since the end of the 1990s, of course, these forms of communication have only become more and more intertwined, but that was absolutely *not* the case for a long while.

We talk in Chapter 6 about the accelerated pace of technological change and its impact on generational tensions. For now, what's important to understand is that the fits and starts with which these technologies came into being, along with fairly slow adoption on the part of 1980s and 1990s consumers, means that the world Old People grew up in continued to be defined by a lack of constant connections. And what *that* means is that all of them—including myself and everyone else in their mid-30s or older—all of them developed their sense of self in a relatively small community. Even for people who grew up in the world's largest cities, their community was essentially a combination of neighborhoods and elementary schools and high schools and summer camps. They had their extended families and the people who worked on the same floor or on the same shift. Those were the *only* people they *ever* came into contact with because it was simply impossible to find people in any other way. They had a few hundred people to choose from, maybe a couple thousand, and that was really it.

And in a world that size, it's comparatively easy to carve out a position for yourself, something that grounds you and assures you that you're noticed. That's the world we were either evolved or designed for. Those of us who grew up in that world may not always have enjoyed the position we found ourselves in, but we at least knew that we had one.

What this means is that the area in which Old People searched for their 150 connections was relatively local. Outside of their extended families, which may have lived in other cities or states, the vast majority of the people closest to them probably lived nearby. It might not have always been easy to find the right personal or professional connections, but the search was characterized by two key factors: You knew where to look, and the population in which you were looking was a relatively small one.

The Search for Connection Goes Global

Now consider the world that Young People grew up in. Every so-called Millennial was no older than 15 in 1995, the year that the Internet became searchable and its use subsequently exploded, and many of your Youngest colleagues were still in single digits. For them, their maturation happened in concert with the exponential adoption of all these new technologies—email, cellphones, texting, online videos, and every other form of communication rapidly converging into a single portal and being utilized by an ever-increasing number of people. For a great many of them, they have literally never known another world.

And here's what *that* means. For your Youngest colleagues—the ones who have *always* had the Internet and dozens or hundreds of television channels to choose from, who have *always* been able to communicate with anyone they wanted to anywhere in the world—for them, their world has *always* been global. It's *always* been 7 billion people large, and it's *never* had any real borders. That might seem like a gift, and in many ways it is.

But when it comes to making meaningful connections and finding a position in the world, a lack of borders is actually a problem. When the entire world is the community that you consider yourself to be a part of, it's much harder to feel like you're being noticed or that what you're doing is interesting, useful, or relevant. In a world with limitless options for connections, when you're sifting through a community of 7 billion, finding the 150 that you can truly attach to is a very difficult task.

What's more, today's Young People have also matured and developed their sense of self in concurrence with an ability that didn't exist for anyone who is now over 35—specifically, the ability to share information about themselves with anyone in the world. Social networking sites became available (and then wildly popular) in the mid-1990s, and viral videos were a possibility well before YouTube's 2005 debut made them almost commonplace. Suddenly, the 7 billion people in your community were all *talking*—and once they started, they never stopped.

First hundreds, then thousands, then millions of people posted snippets of their lives online for the rest of us to view. The diary, which a generation ago was an opportunity for self-reflection and usually intended to be read by the author and no one else, was suddenly transformed into a vehicle for self-expression and intended to be read by as many people as possible. The home movie we shared with our family and friends became an opportunity to get attention and possibly even money from millions of complete strangers. The sheer amount of information about others that is available for our collective consumption beggars comparison. Every day, over 98 *years* of video are uploaded to YouTube—more than 51 million minutes of watchable footage. I'm sure that's as mind-boggling a number to you as it was to me the first time I heard it. People today are being exposed to more information about a greater number of people than has ever before happened in human history.

In Chapter 1 we talked about the "poverty of choice," the phenomenon in which people who are given too many options often choose to do nothing. There is no bigger or better example of that than how the Internet is affecting today's Young People. They want to be connected to others, and they want to be loyal, just as people have always wanted those things. Nothing has changed there. They have simply fallen victim to the most all-encompassing poverty of choice in human history. With all of humanity literally at their fingertips, many Young People are having a harder time than ever deciding where to devote their time, energy, attention, and loyalty.

Moreover, perhaps the most insidious part of the explosive expansion of our global community is the simple fact that people are behaving exactly as they did before such widespread sharing was possible. All of us are constantly engaging in a subtle game of propaganda with our network of family and friends. We selectively share those facts that will get us attention or sympathy or a promotion or the envy of our peers or whatever else we want, and we often choose not to mention anything we believe will paint us in an unflattering light. We've been doing this since the beginning of time—but now it's available on a global scale.

The upshot is this: All day long, since they were old enough to process what they're seeing, today's Young People have been staring at a world that *seems* to be filled with a disproportionate number of people who are richer than they are, or more attractive than they are, or doing more interesting things than they're doing, or doing those things in more exotic places, or living in nicer houses, or driving nicer cars, or becoming overnight successes. Everywhere we look, thousands of people in our global community *seem* to be ahead of us or happier than we are, and every day another 98 years of competition comes online to make our own accomplishments seem that much more unimpressive. The ubiquity of our global community, and our own seeming inability to keep pace, is a constant, crushing pressure inextricably linked to the world we all now belong to.

This is not solely an issue for Young People, of course. Numerous studies have shown a correlation between the amount of time a person spends on social media networks and the likelihood of that person developing symptoms of depression. Every one of us has felt at times as though our own contributions or circumstances are somehow lacking in comparison to what we see online and on television every day. Every one of us has been occasionally paralyzed or overwhelmed by this global poverty of choice. But it's unquestionably worse for today's Young People than for today's Old People because Young People have never had another system. This is the only world they've known. They didn't get a chance to develop very many important relationships before the Internet swept in to interfere. Don't get me wrong: The Internet is an incredible invention, and it has brought us too many advantages to name. But when it comes to the psychological well-being of today's Young People, there are two significant and negative side effects of our Internet-based culture.

First, it has created a world in which our natural desire to attach ourselves to a community has been made infinitely more difficult because there are now an infinite number of places to look for those connections. This helps explain why young Facebook users tend to have hundreds more friends than older people: 27% of 18- to 29-year-old Facebook users have more than 500 friends, while 72% of 65-and-older Facebook users have 100 friends or fewer. This is because those Young People are still trying to find the 150 or so connections that will eventually form their community. This *also* helps explain why today's Young workers have a stated desire to work for a smaller number of companies in their career than Baby Boomers did in theirs. They *want* to find a place to attach to; they *want* to be loyal because there's something in all of us that craves that kind of connection. They may never be able to articulate this sense of loneliness because they don't know there's another way to think. But something in them is hungry for a place to call home, and that desire is borne out in a dozen different ways—from their devotion to social networks and the search for community, to their preference for spending time with friends over almost any other activity, to their hope to work for as few companies as possible.

Second, the Internet has created a culture in which it is alarmingly easy to feel as though our own accomplishments aren't as interesting, valuable, or impressive as the accomplishments of others. Again, this is hardly limited to Young People. It's difficult for all of us to feel like what we're doing is interesting or important when we hold ourselves up against everything that everyone else in the world is doing. But if you developed your sense of self before the Internet truly took hold, then you at least have a foundation to draw strength from. You have a grounding in an earlier and smaller world. *Today's Young People don't.* They know no other way. All they know is they've been dropped into an impossibly large world where everybody is shouting always about everything, and what they want—even if they don't always know how to ask for it—is for somebody to come along and pluck them out of this endless ocean of noise and make them feel like they're not drowning.

So there you have it. Today's Young People are at least as loyal as Young People have been at any time in the past 50 years, and the Internet has created in them a desire to be more loyal than ever. In fact, the biggest problem that your Young colleagues currently face is that they're not entirely certain who they should be loyal to.

And the reasons for *that* are literally everywhere you look.

So if All This Is True, Why Do Young People Seem Less Loyal?

While it might not be true that today's Young People are less loyal than they used to be, there's no denying that it *seems* to be true. Most of us *feel* as though every Young Person we hire is planning to jump ship as soon as possible. I've even heard stories of recent college graduates turning down jobs in favor of moving back home with their parents and not working at all. And a popular 2012 article in *USA Today* highlighted a Young worker who failed to meet his project deadline because it wasn't "convenient" for him. Faced with stories like these, it's no wonder that most of us believe today's Young People simply aren't interested in working hard—or maybe at all.

So why do we feel that today's Young People aren't loyal? The answer is simple. It's not that Young People are less loyal than they used to be. It's that *everyone* is.

And the only proof you need are in the graphs you saw a few pages ago, in Figures 4.1 and 4.2.

It's impossible not to notice in Figure 4.1 that for all male age groups, workplace loyalty seems to have peaked around 1983, only to have fallen off precipitously in the past 30 years, except of course for the Youngest workers. So what happened in the 1980s to negatively impact the loyalty of male workers at almost every age level for the next three decades?

I'm sure you already know the answer. The 1980s introduced a culture of outsourcing and restructuring that over the past 30 years has profoundly altered the nature of the employer–employee relationship. We get into this in more detail in just a moment, but first let's look at a brief history of corporate strategy over the past 70 years, courtesy of *A Brief History of Outsourcing* by Dr. Robert Handfield:

> *Since the Industrial Revolution, companies have grappled with how they can exploit their competitive advantage to increase their markets and their profits. The model for most of the 20th century was a large integrated company that can "own, manage, and directly control" its assets. In the 1950s and 1960s, the rallying cry was diversification to broaden corporate bases and take advantage of economies of scale. By diversifying, companies expected to protect profits, even though expansion required multiple layers of management. Subsequently, organizations attempting to compete globally in the 1970s and 1980s were handicapped by a lack of agility that resulted from bloated management structures. To increase their flexibility and creativity, many large companies developed a new strategy of focusing on their core business, which required identifying critical processes and deciding which could be outsourced. Outsourcing was not formally identified as a business strategy until 1989 (Mullin, 1996). The use of external suppliers for...essential but ancillary services might be termed the baseline stage in the evolution of outsourcing. Outsourcing support services is the next stage. In the 1990s, as organizations began to focus more on cost-saving measures, they started to outsource those functions necessary to run a company but not related specifically to the core business. Managers contracted with emerging service companies to deliver accounting, human resources, data processing, internal mail distribution, security, plant maintenance, and the like as a matter of "good housekeeping." Outsourcing components to affect cost savings in key functions is yet another stage as managers seek to improve their finances.*

To put it in simpler terms, many companies have moved *from* a model that favors growth ("own, manage, and directly control," "broaden corporate bases," etc.) *to* a model that favors efficiency ("increase flexibility and creativity," "identifying critical processes," etc.). In a growth model, employees are a necessary and indispensable piece of the equation; after all, how can you even pretend to be growing if you don't have more and more employees all the time? In an efficiency model, however, employees are an expense that should be managed with the same impartiality that you might use when deciding whether to update your software or scrap your outdated and costly heating system.

But what about professional women? Doesn't their graph (refer to Figure 4.2) tell a different story? On the surface it does. Women have been entering the workforce in greater and greater numbers for the past 40 years, and they are staying in their jobs longer than ever. That is to be commended.

But what should *not* be commended is this: Despite the fact that women are more likely to have a college degree than men (37.1% vs. 34.9% in 2010), they are almost twice as likely as men to work in a part-time capacity (26.6% vs. 13.4%), and they still earn less ($669/week vs. $824/week). Also, because women are more likely to work part time, they're less likely to have workplace benefits. Unfortunately, the rise in female tenure rates also correlates with the increasing desire of businesses everywhere to cut costs wherever possible.

To summarize Dr. Handfield (and also to butcher Rousseau), the social contract between employers and employees has evolved in a way that has made the cultivation of loyalty in the workforce a more difficult issue than ever before.

Why? Because no one will be loyal to you if you are not also loyal to them.

Loyalty Is a Two-Way Street

Loyalty does not exist in a vacuum, nor has it ever. Loyalty doesn't just *happen*. It's a quality that's cultivated, something we prove to each other over and over and over as we move along the spectrum from jobseeker to applicant to new hire to trusted employee to indispensable lynchpin of your company's success. The reciprocal nature of loyalty is one of the easiest things to forget when it comes to dealing with others, but we forget it at our own peril.

This is true in our personal lives as well. If you are married, you will admit that you were not loyal to your husband or wife when you went on your first date together. The loyalty you share developed slowly, over time, as both of you gave each other reasons to want to become a permanent couple. Your children are not loyal to you simply because you adopted or gave birth to them. They develop that loyalty as you feed them and care for them, as you take an interest in their lives and buy them school supplies and comfort them when they have bad dreams and help them decide where to go to college. In everything that we do, loyalty demands proof.

Similarly, if you are loyal to your current employer, it is at least in part because your employer has done things to earn that loyalty. Maybe they've given you a pension or tuition reimbursement or paid vacation. Maybe they kept you on during an unexpected downturn and let you know that they would fight for you when things got tough. Maybe they've guaranteed you a percentage of the profits when your startup finally takes off. Maybe they've done nothing for you that they haven't also done for everyone else they employ. At the absolute minimum, they promised you job security *and then delivered on it.* And as a result, you slowly became a loyal member of the team.[4]

In fact, wherever you find loyal workers, you will *always* find a corporate culture with tangible examples of its determination to earn that loyalty. Consider the military, which is undeniably a system in which loyalty is encouraged and rewarded. While it may be true that a sense of duty and higher purpose animate those who choose to serve, the military itself doesn't rely on noble beliefs to encourage loyalty. It offers educational benefits, pensions after 20 years of service, job placement programs, support groups for family members, discounts on food and other necessities, and several other programs. Those things are part of the reason you still see fifth-generation military families. In much the same way, pensions, flex time, in-building daycare, and other perks are part of the reason employees are loyal to their employers. Wherever you go, loyalty is *always* an earned thing. It's never a given.

---

[4] Conversely, if you don't feel any particular loyalty to your current employer, it is at least in part because they've done things to make you feel that way. We'll be talking about that in a few pages.

Thus, the expectation of immediate loyalty from your newest employees *is completely unrealistic*. They simply have not been around long enough for their loyalty to have been firmly established.

This is not an age-specific thing. There is nothing about being older that inherently makes Old People more loyal than Young People. Former Enron employees of any age were very unlikely to immediately display an unquestioning loyalty to their next employer after watching their life savings disappear. Loyalty is more a function of experience than age, although it so happens that as we get older, we have more time to develop a mutual sense of loyalty with our family, friends, and employers. However, if anything occurs to shake that sense of loyalty, Old people are just as likely as Young ones to become disloyal and unmotivated.

Confirmation of this fact comes from the Center for Work-Life Policy, which found that the proportion of employees professing loyalty to their employers slumped from 95% to 39% between June 2007 and December 2008, while the number of employees who expressed trust in their employers fell from 79% to 22%. Obviously the recession—and, more importantly, the business world's response to it, which in most cases involved punishing rounds of layoffs—had a massively negative impact on worker loyalty. And not just on Young workers. In fact, among all generations surveyed, Baby Boomers exhibited the *highest* levels of discontent with their employers.

In Her Own Words: Ellen H. on Why Loyalty Has Changed

Remember Ellen from the beginning of this chapter? She had a little more to say about how and why loyalty has changed at her company. In her own words:

> I wish I could blame those young managers for abandoning us after we've provided them with such invaluable training, but the truth is it's not their fault. They're being forced to think only about themselves. My company had a phenomenal pension package that we no longer offer to incoming employees—and you can see a direct correlation between the year we stopped offering pensions and our increase in turnover.

These people have to save for their own retirement, and a 5% raise is pretty significant when you think about it over a 20- or 30-year career.

Sadly, even for our remaining pensioned employees, we have seen a major change in their loyalty as well. There is a general consensus that our company is no longer loyal to employees. The need to please Wall Street has taken priority as even longstanding, solid-performing employees are eliminated to reduce operating costs and ensure that Wall Street expectations are exceeded. Promotions are harder to come by and less lucrative than they used to be. Our senior leadership made an ill-advised acquisition a couple years ago, and shortly afterward, the people at my level were told to reduce labor costs in order to offset the loss. That wouldn't have happened 15 years ago. Back then we would have taken the loss without threatening anyone's job security.

It's affected my loyalty to my company as well. I'm now considering early retirement, which I wouldn't have done a few years ago. Unfortunately, I just don't feel like my company cares about me the way it used to, and so I'm having a harder time staying excited about my job.

The evidence is ironclad. If you want loyal and hardworking employees, regardless of their age or experience, you can't just sit idly back and expect it to happen. You have to earn it. If you are dealing with Young People who have not had the chance to see the benefits of being loyal to you, then you'll have to work harder to persuade them than you will with your Older or more-experienced colleagues and employees.

Why all this work? Because if you are the employer, you need to begin this process. You need to show both Young People and Old People that yours is the kind of department or company worth being loyal to. Once you do that, your employees will respond by becoming loyal and giving you all the advantages that loyalty typically confers—dedication, productivity, advocacy to your customers, etc.

So the real question is, are you doing everything you can to prove to others that you deserve their loyalty?

Unfortunately, the answer is probably no.

What We Used to Hear About Work, and What We're Hearing Now

Over the past 85 years, employers have devised several ways to successfully encourage employee loyalty. Here are a couple:

- From 1929 to 1932, at the height of the Great Depression, only 3% of workers with company pensions saw their pensions disappear, and the number of companies that offered pensions actually *increased* by 15%.[5]
- From 1940 to 1960, the number of workers covered by private pensions swelled from 3.7 million to 19 million—fully 30% of the workforce. By 1975 that number had increased again to 40 million, or almost 80% of all employees.

These are the kinds of corporate behaviors that help create a dedicated, hard-working, loyal workforce. When employees know that you'll be there for them through thick and thin, they'll show their appreciation by working harder and looking less often for other jobs. It's as simple as that.

This is the story of the 1930s through the 1970s. Outsourcing didn't exist as a defined business strategy, and so employees didn't worry that their jobs might disappear overnight. Pensions were a firmly established facet of business, and more and more companies offered them as a way to attract the best workers. Real wages were rising all the time. For these and other reasons, employees felt as though their employers actively cared about them, and they repaid their employers with loyalty. There were bumps along the way—most notably recessions, when even the most conscientious employers are sometimes forced to cut staff—but overall the trend during these five decades involved companies providing more and more benefits to their employees, which in turn yielded higher and higher loyalty from those same employees.

---

[5] As we'll soon see, this is a far cry from how the average company handled the recession of 2007–2009.

> ## In Her Own Words: Sharon F. on How Her Company Earned Her Loyalty
>
> Sharon F. is 53 years old and works for a Fortune 100 company. In her own words:
>
> > I work for a company where a significant number of people have never worked for any other company and where their parents, siblings, and children also work. I am one of those people who followed in my father's footsteps and joined the company, where he spent 35 years working. I never planned on working for this company, but it promised the opportunity to make a better living for my family, and I was already familiar with the company, thanks to my father, so I was comfortable with its reputation. I didn't come here because I particularly thought I enjoyed the actual business, but it had provided a good lifestyle for my parents, and I knew it could potentially do the same for me. Over the years, I've found that there are genuinely good people in leadership who care not only about the profits and the future of the business but also about the impact the company has on its employees and customers. I can understand now why my father was happy here for 35 years.

Sharon's story is typical for people her age. When a company goes out of its way to take care of its people, the people respond with loyalty, pride, and hard work.

Since the 1980s, however, the dynamic between companies and their employees has been a markedly different one. The stereotypical picture of the employer–employee relationship that has been handed down to us from the 1950s—ironclad job security, comprehensive benefits, regular raises and bonuses,[6] little if any job hopping—has been replaced. For today's Young People and Old People alike, here are the workplace realities:

---

[6] Often in the form of a holiday ham. Why don't people give meat as bonuses anymore?

- In 2012, Duke's Fuqua School of Business found that almost 75% of respondents indicated labor cost savings as one of the three most important drivers leading to overseas outsourcing, twice the rate of response for any other option. Also, despite the fact that rising labor costs overseas are shrinking the cost gap between employing workers at home vs. workers abroad,[7] only 4% of large companies have any plans to return jobs back to the United States.

- Between August 2000 and February 2004, manufacturing jobs decreased for 43 consecutive months, the longest stretch since the Great Depression. More than 8 million manufacturing jobs have been lost since the 1990s.

- The U.S. Department of Commerce revealed that during the 2000s, America's largest companies (accounting for 20% of all American workers) cut their workforces in the United States by 2.9 million while increasing employment overseas by 2.4 million.

- Inflation-adjusted median household income has decreased every year since 2007. It peaked in 1999 and has not reached that level in the subsequent 15 years.

- In 1983 there were 175,143 pension plans in America; by 2008, there were only 46,926. Also, as recently as 1998, fully 90% of Fortune 100 companies offered defined benefit plans to their new salaried employees. By 2009 that number had fallen to 19%, and by 2013 it was 11%.

- A 2011 Aon Hewitt survey found that of the companies that still offered traditional pension plans, only 44% of those plans were made available to their new hires.

- Twenty-five percent of the jobs in America pay less than $23,050, the federal poverty line for a family of four.

- Since the 1970s, temporary employment has skyrocketed through every kind of economy, from 400,000 a day in 1980 to nearly 3 million by 2000.

---

[7] By 2013, the cost gap between U.S. and China is expected to be only 16%. That means that companies which choose to outsource to China are employing 7 Chinese workers when they could instead be employing 6 U.S. workers for the same overall cost (once shipping, fuel, infrastructure and other costs are factored in).

- The percentage of contract workers in the United States has increased almost 500% since the mid-1980s. Also, 42% of employers planned to hire temporary or contract workers as part of their hiring strategy in 2014, a 14% increase from 2009.

- Of the 8.8 million jobs lost during the 2007–2009 recession, 60% paid between $14 and $21/hour. Of the jobs that have been regained since 2009, only 27% of them pay between $12 and $21/hour. The majority of new jobs (58%) pay less.

This is the working world of today, the one Ellen described in her story, one in which employees have been reimagined as an unwelcome and overpriced expense that should be reduced at every opportunity and with every available tool—or, rather, an expense that *is* being reduced at every opportunity and with every available tool. Unfortunately, the prevailing notion of what work is today is one in which everyone is being expected to fend for themselves. The idea of corporate loyalty is disappearing from the top down because the major incentives that foster employee loyalty—benefits and job security chief among them—are being taken away. Every single one of them. And it is flatly impossible to properly express how big an impact this has on the loyalty of those you work with and lead.

Moreover, the world I've just described is quite literally the only world Young People have ever known. The increasingly disloyal relationship between employer and employee is, for them, the only one that has ever existed.

What Does This All Mean?

This cannot be overstated: Young People have never lived during a time when the business world was trending toward *more* job security, *more* pensions, *more* health benefits, or *more* certainty that their hard work would be repaid in any appreciable form. In fact, virtually all of them began their professional lives after the dot-com bust of the late 1990s, which is when the disappearance of all these incentives really started to accelerate. For them, the *only* world they have ever known has featured layoffs, outsourcing, automation, Enron, and the disappearance of the middle class. It's all they've ever heard—and with the exponential growth of the media, they hear it significantly more often than they would have 10 or 20 years ago. Some of them may even have seen their parents lose their jobs in the name of efficiency, and they're wary of devoting themselves to an employer only to have the same thing happen to them.

In His Own Words: Halal K. on the Rewards of Loyalty

Halal K. is 31 years old and works as a limousine driver for a car service. He was born in Afghanistan, where he began working at the age of 11. His family eventually emigrated to the United States when Halal was 17. In his own words:

When I came to America, I knew no English and had no real education. But my family needed me to work. So I taught myself English and got a minimum-wage job at a sandwich shop. I'd had a strong work ethic instilled in me from a very young age, so I quickly became a store manager, then the manager for six franchises in the area. I did this for eight years, and in that whole time I never thought to look for another job. I liked the work, and I felt important.

Then one day the owner of the franchises I was managing sold them. As soon as the deal was finalized, the new owners told me I had a month to find a new job. Their son wanted my job, so there was no room for me. I'd been loyal and hardworking for eight years, but there was nothing I could do. By this point, I had a wife and three children, and I was about to have no way to support them.

Now I drive limousines. I've been here for two years, and it's all right. They treat me fine. I'm able to take care of my family. But I'm not excited to go to work. I'm just waiting for a new manager or a new owner to come in and put me out on the street again. My current boss tells me that will never happen, but I can't believe him. It's already happened once.

I'm very grateful to be in America, and I wouldn't want anyone to go through what I went through as a child in Afghanistan. The United States is a wonderful country. But I hate the position I'm in right now. I feel powerless.

In His Own Words: Walter C. on the Problem with Handshake Agreements

Walter C. is 33 years old and works as an assistant district attorney. He was hired on at 25 when he completed law school and worked as a state prosecutor for a few years before leaving the government to enter private practice. Now he's back working for the state. In his own words:

> When I was 28, I met an attorney who was thinking about retiring in a few years and was looking for a protégé to train and then sell his business to. At the time, I was disenchanted with public prosecution and was looking for a change. He showed me his company's financials and told me that I'd be able to run the business myself in under three years. So I left the state and started working for him.
>
> Unfortunately for me, we never signed anything. In retrospect, that was a huge mistake on my part, especially considering that I'm a lawyer, but I was young and was inclined to believe this gentlemen. For two years I worked for him, and for two years he taught me very well and seemed to be preparing me to take over his business. He continually talked about his impending retirement.
>
> Then, one day, he apparently decided that he wasn't quite ready to retire. So he presented me with a contract to buy him out of his business that would have guaranteed him a fixed pension for 10 years after the sale. Essentially he wanted to sell me his business and then continue to profit from it after I had purchased it. It was not at all what we had discussed, and every lawyer friend of mine said that it was a ridiculous request on his part and could probably be challenged in court for breach of contract. But then, we hadn't signed a contract, had we?
>
> Ultimately I turned down his offer, and three months later, he fired me while I was on a vacation. I had trusted him with my career, and now I had nothing. I was unemployed for almost a year until I managed to get another job at the state. I will not be entertaining any other offers like his, at least not without signing a lot of papers ahead of time.

In addition, your Young employees are often working on teams with Older colleagues who have more comprehensive benefits than they do—not because the Older ones did anything special to earn those benefits but because those benefits are simply no longer available. Most new hires are entering the workforce with no expectation of ever participating in the various safety nets that many of their Older colleagues are counting on to help sustain them through retirement. When Young People see a company that *used* to offer a variety of benefits to its employees but has decided not to do so anymore, what other conclusion can they reasonably draw than that the company they work for doesn't care as much about its people as it did in the past? How else are they supposed to interpret the rising cost or outright disappearance of employer-sponsored health insurance plans except as an indication that companies aren't as invested in their workforce as they used to be?

If you add all this up, the message that Young People are hearing is that they're supposed to do the same work as everyone else, but they're supposed to do it *for less reward*. What they're hearing is exactly what an Old Person would hear if her boss walked in one day and said, "I'd like you to keep doing the same job you're doing now, but I'm going to pay you 15% less. The economy, you know." It hardly needs to be said that such a conversation would have an immediately negative impact on both her work ethic and her sense of loyalty to that employer.

There are multiple valid arguments to explain why the working world has changed in the ways that it has. The rise of the global economy demanded drastic solutions like outsourcing to reduce operational costs in order to stay internationally competitive. Pensions had to evolve in the face of changing workplace demographics. The elimination of jobs through automation is a natural extension of an effort to keep prices at a level that consumers are willing to pay. All of these statements are true.

But they are also all beside the point. What's important is that an ever-increasing majority of the workforce is being trained to believe that their employers are not going to care about them; and for your Youngest employees and colleagues, that opinion is the only one their experience will justifiably allow.

Make no mistake: Today's Young People *want* to be loyal. We've seen the proof of that already. But they don't enter the workplace as a *tabula rasa* that you can shape as you wish. They enter with preconceptions based on what they've seen and heard, just as people have always done. Unfortunately, what many Young People have seen and heard has caused them to start their professional lives with a deficit of trust. It's a deficit that has been built into them their entire lives and which in most cases has literally nothing to do with anything you have ever specifically said or done to them.

Bottom line: You've got Young People coming in to your company who are simultaneously desperate to belong to something and who have been trained to believe that you're not going to care about them. This explains in large part why they don't immediately display a deep sense of loyalty or the killer work ethic that is loyalty's natural accomplice.[8] They simply don't want to put in a great deal of effort only to find their job outsourced or automated six months down the road. They don't want to start off as a contract worker and give it everything they've got, only to learn that there's not enough money in the budget to turn their contract into a full-time position with benefits. They want to know that they're going to be rewarded for what they do—and in that sense, they are exactly like everyone else.

The point is, if you feel that your workforce is not as loyal or hard working as you'd like them to be, you absolutely *must* consider what messages you're sending to make them feel and act the way they do. Some of the problem is on their shoulders, and we discuss that in Chapter 5. But some of it is also on yours. It's your job to show your employees, both Young People *and* Old People, that what they've seen happening in the world around them is not the way you operate. If you want their loyalty, you have to earn it. That's the way it's always been, and it's more important now than ever before.

---

[8] Part of the reason is because they're lazy and have completely unrealistic ideas about how quickly their careers are likely to advance, which we'll be discussing in greater detail in the next chapter. Don't worry, Young People—your moment is coming!

So What Can You Do?

Hopefully you now appreciate both the reciprocal nature of loyalty and the major reasons workplace loyalty and work ethic seem to be on a steady decline. If so, you might be feeling overwhelmed. After all, the entire working world of the past 30 years seems to be conspiring against you to make finding loyal and hard-working employees all but impossible.

But it's actually much easier than you think.

First, you need to get closer with everyone you work with— Younger or less-experienced and Older or more-experienced people. Remember, the first step to resolving generational issues is to determine all the things Young People and Old People have in common. And when it comes to loyalty and work ethic, we're all on the Us side of the spectrum in several ways.

Qualities, Attitudes and Opinions That Young People and Old People Have in Common

1. All of us, regardless of age or station, want to be loyal to someone or something.

2. All of us, regardless of age or station, want others to be loyal to us.

3. All of us become more or less loyal based upon our experiences. When we can point to concrete instances in which our loyalty has been repaid, we slowly and steadily become more loyal. When we feel as though our loyalty is not being valued, we become slowly and steadily less loyal. In other words, all of us believe that loyalty is something that needs to be earned and can't simply be assumed.

4. All of us are struggling to find reasons to be loyal to our employers because all of us have seen too many instances in which the major incentives that foster loyalty are being taken away.

As you can see, Young People and Old People really aren't that far apart on this issue. We all have the same motivations, and we all respond to our environment in the same way.

Now for the second step—explaining why each generation thinks and behaves the way that it does. Fortunately, when it comes to loyalty, there are very few differences that separate Young People from their Older or more-experienced colleagues, and the reasons for those differences aren't complicated at all.

Key Concepts: Why Your Younger or Less-Experienced Colleagues Think and Behave the Way They Do

1. Today's Young People are actually more interested in building loyal relationships than the Young People of previous generations, in part because they have grown up in a hyper-connected world in which an overload of options has made it more difficult to find and establish a position for themselves. Consequently, they are actively searching for people, companies, and ideas to which they can become loyal.

2. Today's Young People have only ever lived in a time in which the incentives that foster employee loyalty are disappearing, and many of them are wary and skeptical of their employers as a result.

3. Young People have not been working as long as their Older colleagues and so have had less time to determine whether their loyalty to their company will be rewarded.

Key Concepts: Why Your Older or More-Experienced Colleagues Think and Behave the Way They Do

1. Because they have been working for a longer period of time, Old People have had more opportunity to recognize that their loyalty will be rewarded and reciprocated.

2. Today's Old People grew up in a time when employee loyalty was more commonly rewarded, and many of them are still operating with that framework firmly embedded in their minds.

If you can see the several similarities between your Young and Old colleagues, and if you appreciate the reasons that each group thinks and behaves the way they do, then you are well on your way to eliminating loyalty as a divisive issue between the various members of your team, department, and company.

So if one of your Older or more-experienced colleagues has irritated you by expecting you to work harder than you think you've been given a good reason to, try instead to see their persistence for what it really is: that they themselves have been rewarded for *their* hard work, and they believe you will be as well. Or if your Younger or less-experienced colleagues have frustrated you with their apparent disinterest in working hard, try instead to appreciate that they are still uncertain whether loyalty to you or your company actually makes sense. They *want* to be loyal, but they *don't* want to be taken advantage of—any more than you do.

You've heard it said before that people don't leave companies—they leave people. Too many surveys to mention have found that the top two nonfinancial determinants of job satisfaction are a person's relationship with his or her immediate superiors and his or her relationship with immediate colleagues. We *want* to connect with others. All of us, Young People and Old People alike, have a biological imperative to do so. But if all of us only have room in our brain for 150 of those connections, how are you supposed to earn your way onto others' privileged list?

Easy. The same way that our family and friends do it—by caring about colleagues *as people*. If you want to inspire loyalty in others, and if you want them to repay you with hard work, you simply *must* show your employees and coworkers that you care about them as people, not just as pieces in your corporate moneymaking machine. This is true for Young People and Old People alike. If they see you taking an active interest in their lives and career, if they feel you'll go to bat for them when necessary, they'll be loyal to you. If instead they feel that you're using them as a placeholder until you find a better or cheaper alternative, they will repay you by using *you* as a placeholder until they find a better job.

Perhaps your company still offers pensions and comprehensive health insurance. Perhaps you've hired your Young People as full-time employees rather than on a contract or temporary basis. Perhaps your company is well known for having resisted the temptation to outsource dozens or hundreds or thousands of jobs. If so, you're already doing a lot to earn the loyalty you're looking for. But even if you are doing these things—and *especially* if you aren't or can't afford to—there are still a lot of ways to develop your people into loyal, dedicated, and hard-working individuals.

And here are some simple strategies you can use *now*. If you're an Old Person, many of these will help you earn the loyalty of your Younger colleagues. If you're a Young Person, many of these will help you discover the benefits to becoming as loyal as you possibly can. And the best thing is, none of them will cost you a dime.

Ways to Earn Loyalty or Discover Its Value (for the Low Low Price of ZERO DOLLARS!)

- **Present your new hires with business cards on their first day of work.** Or monogrammed t-shirts, or stenciled name-plates, or whatever it is you can think of to let them know that they are a definite part of the team and that you plan on keeping them around for a while.[9]

- **Invite your newest employees or team members to deliver a presentation to the rest of your team on a topic they already know something about.** This will show them that you respect their intelligence and have confidence in their abilities. It will also show the Older or more-experienced people that their Young colleagues are bringing something to the table. If the newest members of your department are able to demonstrate right away that they can be immediate assets, you'll almost certainly foster a strong sense of teamwork more quickly than you otherwise would.

- **Learn their names quickly, call them by name when you say hello, and praise them as often as you can think to.** This will annoy some Old People as unnecessary coddling, but it shouldn't. Older workers often complain about

---

[9] OK, so business cards cost like $8 per million. This one isn't completely free. Sue me.

how needy Young People seem to be and that they're always expecting attention. But honestly, in a world where every traditional incentive for being loyal is under attack, literally the only thing left for Young People to ask for is attention. Is it really so terrible that they want to know you're aware of their existence? More importantly, is it really so hard to give it to them? With job security seemingly more tenuous now than it has ever been, a lack of attention can easily be misinterpreted by inexperienced workers as a prelude to a dismissal.

- **If you are in a supervisory role, tell everyone who directly reports to you, Young and Old alike, that you will go to bat for them if necessary.** This is not a generational issue. Everyone needs to know that the people with whom they have placed their loyalty will fight for them if the need arises. Don't assume that your people know you'll do it. Tell them.

- **Solicit the opinions and ideas of everyone you work with.** Everyone has ideas, and almost all of us want to share them. So when you're updating your website or rolling out a new marketing plan, ask people what they think. All you really need to do is let everyone know that you're listening, even when (as will often be the case) you ultimately decide to go in a different direction than what they've suggested.

- **Give all of your employees, Young and Old, the opportunity to use their skills and abilities on a regular basis.** A 2012 SHRM report on job satisfaction found that having opportunities to use their skills and abilities was *more* important to most professionals than either job security or overall compensation. When people have a chance to showcase their talents, they feel both accomplished and valued, and they'll want to continue working in a place where they can keep feeling that way. If you don't know what skills and abilities your people would like to use, you're going to have to ask them.

- **Invite your colleagues and employees to lunch on a weekly or monthly basis.** Again, you can do this with both Young People and Old People. Doing so will make them feel more connected to you, and that is the central building block of loyalty. Besides, you might end up finding out that they have some useful skills you never would have known about if you hadn't spent those few minutes in the cafeteria with them.

- **Ask your Older or more-experienced colleagues why they have stayed with your company as long as they have.** You'll probably get some flippant answers like, "Because they pay me," or "I couldn't find anything better," but eventually you should start to hear the kinds of things you need to hear: "It's a good company," "They kept my job open when I was sick for seven months," "I like the people I work with." If your Older colleagues have been given reasons to be loyal, there's a good chance that you'll be given the same reasons yourself, provided that you stay long enough. And if you're trying to earn the loyalty of your Younger colleagues, taking the initiative to share your own reasons for being loyal will almost certainly help generate a similar loyalty in your Young People.

- **If you are a supervisor or manager, ask your employees what they want out of their job *over and above* the salary and benefits your company provides.** Fewer than 40% of employers ever ask this question of their employees, young or old. How can you hope to know what really motivates your people if you never ask? The common failure to ask this question is a central reason there's often a large disconnect between what employ*ers* think is important—which is generally salary and benefits—and what employ*ees* think is important, which is generally salary, benefits, and whatever psychological benefit they gain by working in your industry, at your company, or for you in particular. You will *never* know what those things are unless you ask, and if you don't know, you can't inspire loyalty as much as you'd like to.

- **Offer your services as a mentor or create a mentorship program.** In 2006 Sun Microsystems released the results of a five-year study of more than 1,000 of its employees who had participated in a mentoring program, either as a mentor or mentee. If you'll allow that retention rates are a decent barometer of loyalty, then it looks like mentoring programs are a phenomenal way to improve loyalty; 72% of mentees and 69% of mentors were still working for Sun after five years, compared to 49% of employees who hadn't participated in the program. Oh, and both mentors and mentees were also promoted *five to six times more often* than those who didn't participate. Consider that if making more money sounds nice.[10]

- **Tell your manager or other senior employees that you intend to spend your career working your way up the ladder at your company.** New employees rarely think to say something like this because it's impossible to know what will happen; you could move or go back to school or start your own business or get a job offer you simply can't turn down. But while you can't know the future, that doesn't mean you can't express your desire to be loyal right now. Doing so will almost certainly impress the people you're probably trying to impress. Then all you'll need to do is back up your words with actions.

---

[10] One of the surprising findings of the Sun study was that the mentoring program was *least* effective for the highest performers. This seems counterintuitive, but the researchers concluded that "the better investment for Sun would be to spend their [resources] on lower performers to help them raise their level of performance."

Remember, the people you work with, Young People and Old People, want to be loyal. They're looking for it. All you need to do is give them reasons to believe that their loyalty won't be misplaced, and you'll soon find yourself with a more loyal and more productive workforce than you've ever thought possible.

And that, I believe, is everything that needs to be said about the nature of loyalty and its effect on work ethic. Congratulations on making it this far! You've now survived the longest chapter in the book. From this point forward, you are much less likely to do that thing where you flip through the next several pages to see how close you are to the end of the chapter and get increasingly annoyed as you realize it's farther away than you want it to be.

Hopefully you've seen that the fundamental drivers of loyalty aren't really generational issues at all. On these points, Young People and Old People are actually quite similar—which means that the strategies that work for one group will often work just as effectively for the other.

If you are an Old Person, you may have noticed that you're being asked to do a little more than your Younger or less-experienced colleagues. The reason for this is simple: Employers must be the ones who create an environment conducive to fostering loyalty, and employers are almost by definition Older or more-experienced than the people they're employing. However, in Chapter 5, it will be Young People who end up having to do more, for reasons that will make perfect sense very shortly. See? It all evens out, which is the way it has to be if we're going to solve all these generational issues once and for all.

And why will Young People be shouldered with such a burden? Because Old People tend not to expect to become CEO after three weeks on the job, but some Young People do. It's undeniable that many Young People have completely unreasonable expectations when it comes to how long and hard they'll have to work in order to move up through the ranks, and their approach to career advancement is probably one of your major sources of generational tension. If the quiz in Chapter 3 revealed you to be an Old Person, then we'll be talking about why your Younger or less-experienced colleagues think the way they do and what you can do to set them straight.

But if you happen to be a Young Person, then get ready for a healthy dose of reality. Your moment of truth approaches!

Key Strategies for Resolving Issues with Your Younger or Less-Experienced Colleagues

1. Present your new hires with business cards on their first day of work.

2. Invite your newest employees or team members to deliver a presentation to the rest of your team on a topic they already know something about.

3. Learn their names quickly, call them by name when you say hello, and praise them as often as you can think to.

4. If you are in a supervisory role, tell everyone who directly reports to you that you will go to bat for them if necessary.

5. Solicit the opinions of everyone who directly reports to you on a regular basis.

6. Invite your colleagues and employees to lunch on a weekly or monthly basis.

7. If you are a supervisor or manager, ask them what they want out of their job *over and above* the salary and benefits your company provides.

8. Offer your services as a mentor or create a mentorship program.

9. Give them the opportunity to use their skills and abilities on a regular basis.

Key Strategies for Resolving Issues with Your Older or More-Experienced Colleagues

1. If you are in a supervisory role, tell everyone who directly reports to you that you will go to bat for them if necessary.

2. Solicit the opinions of everyone who directly reports to you on a regular basis.

3. Invite your colleagues and employees to lunch on a weekly or monthly basis.

4. Ask them why they have stayed with your company as long as they have.

5. If you are a supervisor or manager, ask your employees what they want out of their jobs *over and above* the salary and benefits your company provides.

6. Give them the opportunity to use their skills and abilities on a regular basis.

7. Tell your manager or other senior employees that you intend to spend your career working your way up the ladder at your company.

5

On The Pace of Career Advancement
(In Any Career)

If for any reason you chose to stop reading at this point,[1] you would walk away from this book with everything you need to know to create the kind of workplace culture that will inspire loyalty in everyone, Young People and Old People alike.

However, having a *loyal* workforce in no way guarantees that you'll have a *productive* workforce. Loyalty plays an enormous role in determining whether your colleagues and employees are interested in working hard, but it's not the only factor. When it comes to instilling a killer work ethic in your company, department, or team, a more important question you'll have to answer is whether your people actually want to be productive in the first place.

If you've never complained about a colleague's subpar work ethic, then you've probably spent your entire career working alone. But even then, you were almost certainly assigned to group projects in high school and occasionally whined to your parents that you were doing all the work, while your worthless classmates just screwed around and got the same grade you did.

You've probably done the same with a few of your professional peers as well. But a curious thing happens when we feel as though our colleagues aren't putting in the same effort we are. If those people are roughly our age, we usually resign ourselves to the fact that some people just work harder than others. However, when we're complaining about a lack of work ethic in people who are significantly Older or Younger than we are, our logic starts to shift.

---

[1] I don't know why you would want to do this, but possible reasons include "lost will to live" or "unexpectedly became illiterate."

That logic can best be summarized by the following two stories:

In His Own Words: Barry R. on the Work Ethic of the Young

Barry R. is 51 years old and works in the material handling industry, which supplies forklifts and other warehousing solutions equipment. He has worked in this industry for over 20 years and is currently frustrated by the attitude of many of his company's recent hires. In his own words:

> We have added a number of twenty-somethings to our workforce this year, and while we don't experience this phenomenon with all of them, in almost every case where we have hired a person with a degree (especially in sales and operations roles), their patience with "time in the job" and "paying their dues" and their commitment to doing a great job first in order to earn the respect of their peers and thus be able to earn advancement is woefully and painfully short. I know this is a stereotypical trait of the "Millennials" and we thought we were forewarned and were watching for it, but it has amazed and overwhelmed some of my managers.

> I don't want to generalize, but it appears they have been programmed by someone (guidance counselors, teachers, parents?) into believing that they are entitled to five-day, 8-to-5 workweeks and wages approaching six figures just because they have a college degree. Commitment and dedication to a job do not seem to carry the same level of weight with them as do their commitments to their social media circles.

> Here's an example. We recently hired two young men, ages 25 and 24, who had both come from less-than-wonderful hourly jobs and who both seemed grateful and excited to be working for us during their three-month training period. They even said the right things as they moved into their initial work assignments. But within four months of being on the job, they both wanted to know what their "next steps" were and when they would be considered for management roles. Both of them also seemed to adopt semi-superior attitudes and were neither shy nor careful about expressing their disdain for their

elders who were not as e-device savvy or as "connected" as they were. This did not make them any friends.

We still have these two young men with us, and we are working to make sure there are connections between what they produce and what they earn and that we are able to show them career paths—but we are concerned that their impatience and their need for instant gratification will prevent them from sticking it out.

In His Own Words: Randall O. on the Work Ethic of the Old

Randall O. is 33 years old and works in logistical support for a warehousing firm. Although he and Barry work in similar industries—Barry's company makes the kind of products that Randall uses daily—the two men don't know each other and have no business connection to one another. However, Randall shares Barry's frustration, albeit in a different direction. In his own words:

There is an older gentleman I work with right now who is going to be retiring in a few months, and he is totally coasting until that date. We are supposed to be at work at 8:30 every day, but he usually rolls in around 9 at the earliest and often after. Therefore, other people, including myself, have to cover for him sometimes until he gets here. Even though we work "behind the scenes," we still deal with customers face-to-face sometimes, and often his customers are left wondering where he is. Then once he is here, he will disappear for a while and no one will know where he's gone. He'll run errands or take long lunches. Most people would feel bad, but not this guy. He's got one foot out the door and isn't going to look back once he's gone. Personally, I don't care if he's only got a few months left. If this is how he's going to act, they should just fire him and replace him with somebody we can count on. He can keep his retirement or pension or whatever he's got lined up; I just want him to stop making my life difficult because he can't be bothered to do his job anymore.

There's a good chance you've felt like Barry or Randall, or possibly both of them. It's easy to imagine anyone with a few years' experience echoing Barry's comments, and it's easy to imagine an 18-year-old new hire parroting Randall's frustration. Older or more-experienced people are forever accusing their Younger or less-experienced colleagues of idleness, laziness, and unreasonable expectations, and Young People continually criticize their elders for resting on their laurels and doing as little as necessary to keep their jobs. Ironically, when it comes to this particular element of generational discord, each side is blaming the other for exactly the same thing—not working hard enough.

You'll also notice that there are only two versions of these stories rather than four. That's because if you're a so-called Traditionalist, you don't have one criticism about the work ethic of Millennials and a different criticism about the work ethic of Gen Xers; as far as you're concerned, they're all just young and lazy. And if you're a Millennial or Gen Xer, you don't have different problems with your Baby Boomer and Traditionalist colleagues because to you they're all determined to twiddle their thumbs for the rest of their careers. The two-generation model strikes again!

So what you're really dealing with is the same issue interpreted from two distinct points of view. However, that does not mean the issue of work ethic is perfectly balanced between lazy Young People on the one hand and burned-out Old People on the other. The issue of stagnant and enervated Older workers is undoubtedly real and one we address later in this chapter. But hardly anyone would argue that the far greater problem is the tsunami of Young People who just flat-out don't seem interested in working hard. We've talked about how the nature of today's employer–employee relationship has, in many cases, negatively influenced Young People's attitude toward work in general and toward their employers in particular. But if you're doing everything you can to give them a place to belong, and if you're providing them with solid reasons to be loyal to you, why are so many of them still under the delusion that they can show up to work whenever they feel like it? And why do *any* of them expect to be promoted four months after getting hired?

There are two main reasons that the Young People you're working with today seem to have such an anemic work ethic. The simplest answer is also one of the easiest things in the world to overlook: The Older colleagues you currently work with are the ones that *either* demonstrated a healthy work ethic from the beginning *or* figured out the importance of a strong work ethic very, very quickly. If you could look back at everyone hired into your company in 1950 or 1975 or 1992, you'd almost certainly find a collection of people with varying work ethics, just like you're finding today. The ones who were willing and eager to work hard have stuck around and been promoted and otherwise advanced in their professions; the ones who *weren't* willing or eager to work hard have long since been fired or otherwise been encouraged to seek opportunities elsewhere. So, quite simply, if you're an Old Person, the reason your same-age peers often seem to possess a uniformly solid work ethic is because the ones who didn't have a good work ethic aren't around anymore to skew the numbers.

The second reason, however, takes a little longer to explain. Many of today's Young People are operating under a false assumption, one they've inherited in part because of the technological world they've grown up with. If you're an Old Person trying to figure out how to instill a first-rate work ethic in your Younger or less-experienced colleagues, you'll soon know what to say to them.

And if you're a Young Person, I'm about to tell it to you myself.

A Secret About Every Old Person You Work With

This section is written specifically with Young People in mind, but everyone should read it.

Young People, I know that part of the problem you sometimes have with your Older colleagues is that you feel like they're in your way. Even if you don't want to admit it, part of you thinks they're accidentally or maliciously blocking your forward progress. That's not exactly a fair way to think, but it's not unreasonable, either. If it's any consolation, every one of *them* sometimes felt the same way when they were in your position.

Which leads us to the secret about every Old Person you work with, one you need to fully understand. Brace yourselves...

They weren't always Old People.

I know how difficult that is for you to believe. After all, they've always looked like Old People to you. If there happens to be an Old Person nearby,[2] do yourself a favor and stare at them for a bit. Note the crow's feet around the eyes, the receding or non-existent hairline, the bifocals and walking canes and daily cocktail of medications, the stooped shoulders and jowly cheeks. They're so old! And for as long as you've known them, they've always been old.

However, that just isn't true. They weren't always Old People; they *changed into* Old People, slowly and over time. Naturally, you understand this, but it's surprisingly easy to forget, the same way all of us have forgotten what it really and truly is like to be 5 or 8 or 13 years old.

But enough talk. A picture is worth a thousand words, and so the best way to illustrate the fluid nature of the life that your Older or more-experienced colleagues have lived is to allow you to compare what I look like today (left) ...with what I looked like in my 9th-grade yearbook photo (right):

---

[2] If there isn't, you can probably find one at a nearby golf course or your local Cadillac dealership.

I'll give you a moment to let these two images sink in.

The one on the left is presentable, right? I'd argue that I look at least modestly competent. I'm reasonably well dressed. Based only on this photo, it's not entirely inconceivable that a company that chose to hire me might not completely regret the decision to do so.

However, there's no disputing that my 9th-grade photo is a complete atrocity. It's impossible to fully enumerate all the bad decisions I had to make simultaneously in order for you to have this photograph to look at. Your eyes will no doubt have first been drawn to my hair, that rakishly lopsided Vanilla Ice pompadour that gives my head the vague anvil shape that was exactly as appealing to women back then as it is today.[3] You might forgive the awkward expression on my face as the sadly unavoidable consequence of adolescence. But nothing can forgive that *partial* mullet I was rocking in the back. Even if you condemn the mullet in all its forms, you should at least concede the confident bravado required to wear one. Alas, I couldn't quite get there. Instead of a party in the back, mine was more of a quiet get-together. Oh, and that chain I'm wearing? Suspended at the bottom is a dragon claw holding a crystal ball. I couldn't make that up even if I wanted to, and why on Earth would I want to? I suppose I could argue that I was simply 20 years ahead of my time—after all, *Game of Thrones* is really popular right now, and it has plenty of dragons—but my anvil-shaped semi-mullet sort of kills that argument before it gets off the ground. As you might have already guessed, my 9th-grade girlfriend was imaginary.

However, over the past two decades, I've slowly and steadily gotten better. In that sense, I am much like a fine cheese.

Experience, Experience, Experience

And just as I have changed over the years, so have all the Old People you work with. This leads to the first point about the nature of

---

[3] I spent about 40 minutes every morning on that hairdo, by the way. Repeat: For well over a year, I spent 40 minutes every morning—consciously, meticulously, and intentionally making myself look this bad.

career advancement that you absolutely *must* understand if you hope
to have a happy and successful professional life:

None of the Older people you work with got where they are overnight.

This sounds like such an obvious statement that it hardly needs
to be said, but it does. If you're relatively new at your company, then
all of your Older colleagues seem to have simply always *been there*,
doing the same jobs today that they've been doing forever. But that
isn't true. They've spent years working their way into their current
positions, if not at your company then somewhere else, slowly building the skill set necessary to do the jobs they're currently doing. Years.
Not days, not weeks, not months—*years*.

If you're a typically ambitious Young Person, or if you're currently
less experienced than many of the people you work with and eager to
be taken more seriously, then you're probably fairly confident that
you already have everything you need to run things yourself. That
supreme belief in our skills and abilities is one of the foundational
qualities of youth. I thought it myself when I was younger, as did
each and every one of your Older colleagues, although many of them
will have forgotten that they used to think that way; indeed, forgetting how we used to think plays a definite role in generational tensions because as we age we become progressively less and less able to
empathize with our Younger or less-experienced colleagues.

However, even if it's somehow true that you are the most capable,
competent, and intelligent person at your company, you can't prove
that to anyone without some experience behind you. Career advancement is exclusively a function of *experience*, not age, although the
two often go hand in hand given the process of gaining experience
necessarily involves getting older. It's not always a perfect correlation,
however, and there are myriad examples, most notably in the technology sector, where the most-experienced individuals are significantly
Younger than the people they employ. This can be a problem for Old
People, who sometimes feel that age necessarily confers seniority and
that they therefore deserve to occupy the most important positions.
With rare exceptions, though, people are in the positions they're in
because of their experience, not their age.

But I'm getting ahead of myself. A moment ago I allowed for the possibility that Young People might actually know everything there is to know about the companies or industries where they work, and that just isn't true. Not only that, but if you're a Young Person, you also don't know as much as the people who've been there a decade longer than you have.

You don't have to take my word for it, though.

The 10,000-Hour Rule (Which Is a Lie but Gets the Point Across Anyway)

In his book *Outliers*, Malcolm Gladwell popularized the notion that 10,000 hours is the amount of time it takes to become an expert in something. For those of you who haven't read it, he based his hypothesis on the work of psychologist K. Anders Ericsson, who, along with two colleagues,[4] studied violin students at Berlin's Academy of Music. The students were divided into three groups: those who had been judged by their teachers to have world-class potential, those considered good enough to play professionally but not at an elite level, and those considered incapable of achieving professional-level success.

Here's what they found:

Students who would end up as the best in their class began to practice more than everyone else: six hours a week by age nine, eight by age 12, 16 a week by age 14, and up and up, until by the age of 20 they were practicing well over 30 hours a week. By the age of 20, the elite performers had all totaled 10,000 hours of practice over the course of their lives. The (second tier) students had totaled, by contrast, 8,000 hours, and the (third tier) just over 4,000 hours.

As you can see, Ericsson and colleagues found a direct correlation between practice and proficiency—in other words, practice really does seem to make perfect. Based on these findings, Gladwell argued that 10,000 hours is the magic number of time required to become

---

[4] Who are probably annoyed that nobody knows their names, by the way.

an expert at anything, and now we all repeat it as though it's a definitive answer. In fact, if you Google "How long does it take to become
an expert?" the first thing that pops up is a giant **10,000 hours**, as
though that's all there is to it. According to Gladwell, five years of full-
time dedication to a given skill will make anyone an expert.

So you should be running your company after five years, right?

Unfortunately, this conveniently simple solution suffers from a
few problems. First, the 10,000-hour answer completely ignores the
effect of natural talent. The students in Ericsson's study, for example,
had been presorted by their music teachers in terms of natural ability.
The "expert" group had already been identified as having the potential to become experts, while the third group had already been identified as lacking that potential. Although it's certainly possible that
practice and determination might permit anyone to become a world-
class violinist, it's also true that those people might have to practice
more than 10,000 hours to do so—or that musical prodigies might
have to practice less. It also doesn't take into account any physical or
genetic factors that might play a part in determining expertise. I could
spend all the time in world perfecting my basketball skills, but I'm
5'11", and it's difficult to imagine any level of commitment on my part
that would overcome the fact that most NBA players could block my
shots without having to jump.

Second, Gladwell's insistence that 10,000 hours is invariably the
threshold of expertise also overlooks the fact that some skills are
more complicated to master than others. Becoming a world-class
neurosurgeon, for example, is just plain harder to do than becoming
a champion poker player. In fact, others have actually gone to the
trouble of attempting to calculate the amount of time necessary to
achieve expertise in a variety of fields, and the answers vary considerably—7,680 hours for poker players, 13,440 for chefs, 700 for yoga,
9,600 for sports, 15,360 for computer programming, and 42,240 for
neurosurgery. Thus, the skill you're attempting to master has a significant effect on how long you'll need to spend on it to master it.

Third, the idea of achieving expertise simply by powering through
10,000 hours of practice doesn't take into consideration the *quality*
of that practice. Without the proper coaching or studied reflection,
practice doesn't lead to improvement. You might advance to a certain

point simply by doing the same thing over and over again, but you're unlikely to become an expert unless you're analyzing your progress, experimenting with new approaches, and studying the success of recognized experts in your field. That's the reason professional athletes have coaches, and it's the reason that having a mentor is critical if you want to reach the upper echelons of any business.

So Gladwell's 10,000-hour rule is hardly perfect. Some people might advance more quickly than you because they have greater natural aptitude than you do, because they chose an easier path than you did, or because they have devoted more time to analyzing their progress than you have. Because all three of these factors are working simultaneously but to different degrees within each of us, it's fairly difficult to state conclusively that my five years' experience should be more highly valued than your four years' experience.

However, the *idea* is sound—that is, we get good at things because we spend time working on them. As long as we put in the time to learn from our failures, analyze our successes, and push to become better, then all of us have an inevitable tendency to actually get better. In the broader sense that concentrated practice is the key to advancement, Gladwell and Ericsson's 10,000-hour rule is as useful a number as Dunbar's 150 is for the number of people you can actively care about at any given time. You might be able to master your craft in 8,000 hours if you're naturally gifted at it, you might need only 5,000 if it's a fairly easy skill to master, and you might take 14,000 if you've chosen something more difficult or don't have the right coaches to help you along. But no matter what your particular circumstances, you should expect to devote a *lot* of time to getting good at whatever you want to get good at, whether it's perfecting your slap shot or earning accolades in your career.

And you know what that means for you, Young People?

Advancement Is a Process

Yes, Young People, advancement is a process. This is probably the most important thing to understand if you want to resolve any generational tensions related to career advancement, and it is an essential concept to understand and internalize if you want to have a happy and successful career. Advancement is a *process*, not a *right*. We do not *get* promotions or awards or raises the way that we *get* presents. We *earn* promotions and awards and raises. We earn them as a result of our experience, and the only way to accumulate that experience is slowly and methodically, the way that all your Older or more-experienced colleagues have done.

Unfortunately, "slowly and methodically" is not a speed Young People generally enjoy. Not only do Young People typically prefer things to move more quickly than Old People, but the notion of slow and steady progress runs counter to the rapid-fire pace of the modern world. We talk more about that in a few pages, but for now, it needs to be said that your career advancement won't be slow because your Older or more-experienced colleagues are insisting on it.

Rather, advancement is a slow process because that's its nature—not just with your career, but with everything that we do.

Your answers to the following two questions should help you convince yourself.

Quiz: Show Me The Money!!!

1. How do most professional athletes become professional athletes?

A. They ask really nicely.

B. Their parents gave them cool first names like Plaxico and D'Brickashaw, thus guaranteeing their eventual stardom.

C. They train constantly, endure injuries, analyze countless hours of game film, eat a depressingly tiny amount of french fries, travel continuously, and I could go on.

D. They're really good at all the Madden games.

2. How do most professional musicians become professional musicians?

A. They practice, write, record, and tour constantly—like the Beatles, who played at least 1,200 shows in Germany between 1960 and 1964, the majority of which were attended by people who probably didn't know who The Beatles were.

B. They live near a record shop.

C. They experiment with heroin.

D. They watch a *lot* of music videos on VH1 and YouTube.

The answers are obvious—and this is how advancement happens in *everything we do*. Some people have a natural gift for athletics, others for music, others for sales, and others for management. Some people work harder than others. Some people have better access to educational resources than others. Some few people are even luckier than others. And perhaps you've been privileged enough to have all of these factors working in your favor. Perhaps you're the smartest, hardest-working, luckiest, and most innately talented member of your entire company. But *even if that's true*, you still can't expect to advance without dedicating countless hours of time to honing and perfecting all of those natural gifts. In the history of professional football, nobody has ever picked up a football for the first time and immediately started playing in the NFL. In the history of music, nobody has ever picked up an instrument and immediately played complete songs to an enthralled audience at a packed amphitheater. And in the history of business, nobody has ever been an overnight success, despite what you read online.

The point is, you have to practice *everything* in order to get good at it. That's why we tend not to marry people immediately after going on a great first date, although you can definitely do it in Vegas if you want to. But you shouldn't, and your friends will make fun of your poor decision making if you do. The development of a healthy relationship takes time, and there's no shortcut for that. You have to practice video games before you can beat online opponents, languages before you become fluent, recipes before you can perfect them, home improvement projects before you can finish them as well as a contractor might have, and even parenting before you start to feel like you really know what you're doing. Everything we do requires time, dedication, and practice. It's as simple as that.

Young People, when it comes to your career, you simply *must* realize that a career is not a separate kind of experience from the other experiences in a person's life. A career is simply another experience—an experience that requires the same things as all the other experiences we ever have. We start, we learn, we improve, we screw up a few times, we learn from our mistakes—and if we're smart and focused and don't quit, and then we continually move forward.

Again, advancement is a process. And when it comes to your Older or more-experienced colleagues, the simple fact is that they've been going through that process longer than you have. There will always be a few incompetent people in positions of authority who owe their success more to luck or family connections than anything else, but those cases are the exception rather than the rule. In the overwhelming majority of cases, your Older or more-experienced colleagues are where they are because they've worked extremely hard to get there.

In Her Own Words: Karen F. on Career Advancement

Karen F. is 63 years old and works for a Fortune 500 company. At the time she shared this story, she was planning to retire in 6 months. Upon reflecting on her own career trajectory, here's what she had to say:

I never thought I'd get to this point. I will have been with my current company for 24 years when I retire, and I had no intention of ever even working for them. I graduated from college with a degree in education and went to work as a high school teacher for 5 years. I left teaching for 6 years to stay home and raise my three children, and I might have done that forever if I'd been able to. But a divorce demanded that I return to work, so I returned to teaching for another 8 years. I might have done *that* forever if I'd been able to as well, but eventually the financial reality of trying to raise three children on a teacher's salary forced me to look for a job with higher earning potential. That's how I ended up where I am today.

Actually, that's how I ended up at my current company. Where I am today takes a little longer to explain. I came into my company in the sales department but was transferred 8 months later to direct mail. I worked there for 2 years then took a job first in marketing and then agency. Both of those positions lasted for just over a year. I then landed in public affairs, where I've been for the past 16 years. I've had 8 different titles in public affairs, so an average of 2 years per promotion. Some happened in less than a year, while others took 4 years.

I love what I do now, and I find the work very rewarding. But the entire journey hasn't been perfect. I've held jobs doing work that I found positively mind-numbing. But I learned several things early on. First, if you come to work, do your job, and stay away from the gossip-mongers and the complainers, you will be noticed. There are times I didn't think this was accurate because there's also the "squeaky wheel gets the grease" theory, and I saw my share of self-promoters moving to new and exciting positions. But that just wasn't my personality, so I went with my comfort level. It took time to see the results of being patient. What I learned later on is that it takes time to build your reputation as someone who can be placed anywhere, learn the new work, and do a good job. Some of the self-promoters quickly fizzled out and became pigeonholed because they had spent so much time trying to convince people they were amazing that they hadn't spent enough time actually being amazing. Meanwhile, those of us who chose to do our job, pay attention to detail, and add value, not only to our own work but look for opportunities to add value to others, were rewarded.

One example for me was when I was asked to lead a team that was preparing for what was, at the time, the great unknown called Y2K. No one knew what would happen to computer systems in the year 2000, and there was great fear at the time that all systems would shut down. So even though I had absolutely no experience with computers nor any particular interest in them, it was presented to me as a promotion to a leadership position, so I accepted. The belief was that I could learn what I needed to know because I had demonstrated with each of my previous roles that I would take the time to learn the work and then work hard to complete it successfully.

I'm now a senior director for my company, a position I've held for the past 6 years. In that capacity, I have sat at tables with most of the CEOs of the Fortune 100. I've met two U.S. presidents, been invited to dinner in the White House, and attended an official signing in the Oval Office. I don't say these things to brag because quite honestly I don't care very much about honors and awards. I only mention it because I would never in a million years have thought my career would take me where it did. That would be my message to anyone reading this. You simply never know where your career is going to take you. If you stay focused and do a great job, you'll be rewarded in ways you can't even imagine today. It just might take a little longer than you wish it did.

Karen's specific experience might be unique to her, but the long and unpredictable path her career has taken absolutely isn't.

This isn't to say that your Older colleagues always have the best ideas or that their greater experience is always the best guide for determining how to address new business practices or disruptive technologies; we discuss those issues in more detail in the next chapter. Right now, though, what's important to understand is that all the people you work with who have been with your company longer than you have earned their way into the positions they're in today. They've done it through a combination of hard work, study, perseverance, trial and error, collaboration with their peers, stubborn refusal to quit, and the occasional injection of dumb luck. They've powered through some difficult times, and in some cases they've encountered and overcome existential threats to your company's survival. They might not often talk about those moments because the people who do can be just as annoying as that friend of yours who won't shut up about his glory days playing high school football. But they've worked *hard* to get where they are, and they deserve respect for that.

And Now, Something for Old People

We've now explained to Young People why their Older or more-experienced colleagues are where they are, how they got there, and how they themselves will get there in the future. If you are Young or relatively inexperienced compared to your colleagues, this should help you see Old People in a different and healthier light. With respect to career advancement, the business world is operating just as it always has. Unlike with our evolving pension and healthcare systems, Old

People are not taking advantage of benefits that today's Young People don't have access to. The path to career advancement is a process, the same as it's always been, and Old People have typically been going through that process longer than Young People. Hopefully this realization will help reinforce the notion that when it comes to career advancement, all of us are far more Us than Them.

However, if you're generally Older or more experienced than your colleagues, then you've probably been reading the last few pages with a fair amount of incredulity. *"Advancement is a process? You have to put in some time before your efforts are going to be rewarded? Of course!!! Who in the world doesn't already know this?"* If you've experienced any amount of generational tension with your Younger or less-experienced colleagues, a lot of it probably has had to do with your frustration that you even have to talk about this issue in the first place.

So we're now going to discuss two concepts that will mitigate this frustration. The first will explain why the concepts of hard work and delayed gratification seem to have become more difficult for today's Young People to grasp than they may have been for you, and the second will remind you that it's not only Young People who suffer from an occasional aversion to hard work.

But first things first: Why do we even need to talk about the nature of career advancement and the importance of hard work? Isn't this stuff so obvious that we shouldn't need to have a conversation about it? The answer should be yes, but it isn't. To understand the reason for that, we're turning once again to our recent technological revolution in general and the Internet in particular, both of which have given many Young People a misconception about the nature of advancement.

The One Thing Technology Can't Improve

I'm certain that while I write this paragraph, I'm going to screw something up. There will be a word I don't like, or a phrase, or maybe I'll realize halfway through that I'm just not saying things the way I want to. So I'll mash my pinky finger on the Backspace key and start over like nothing happened. Fifty years ago, I would have had to rip an entire page out of my typewriter and begin from the top. Five hundred years ago, I would have just ruined a piece of parchment worth more than some houses. And five thousand years ago, I would have defaced an entire cave wall—which I could probably have erased by chiseling out the entire offending section, but *man* does that sound tedious.

There is absolutely no question that technology has improved our lives in almost every imaginable way. We can eat foods our ancestors didn't know existed, and we can grow that food with a confident certainty they never experienced. We can travel distances that not too long ago were literally inconceivable. We can encode information on *light beams*, which I am doing right now and which is still so bewildering to me that I sometimes think it's all just magic. Our technology is so ubiquitous and has been demonstrated to improve so many areas of our daily lives that it's tempting to believe it can do everything. Need to cure a disease? Engineer a drug. Want to meet the love of your life? Use a computer algorithm that matches people according to their preferences. Interested in living a few hundred years? There are people working on that. Whether they're successful or not remains to be seen, but the very fact that some people think it's even possible suggests that there's no limit to what technology can accomplish.

But there is. Because despite its myriad miracles, technology simply does not and *cannot* improve *the rate at which we acquire knowledge or develop skills.* There is no machine that can turn you into a doctor in six months; there is no software program that can shortcut your path from piano owner to concert performer. Nothing we have developed, and nothing we are going to develop in the foreseeable future, can accelerate the process by which you learn an instrument or master a language, excel at a sport, or become a world-class parent. Start, practice, fail, learn, practice, fail, learn, repeat—for the entirety of human history, that is the *only* solution we've ever come up with. If a given skill required 1,000 hours of study in the past, that same skill requires 1,000 hours of study today. Some people learn more quickly than others, some people practice more than others, and some people have a greater natural aptitude for a certain skill than others. But technology simply *can't* do anything to help.

Our technology has made *access* to knowledge infinitely easier than it was in the past. The Internet has placed the entire wealth of human knowledge at our fingertips. When I was younger, I had to go to the library to find information, and then only after wading through the swampy morass of the Dewey decimal system could I hope to find a book that might maybe be useful. Now everything—literally *everything*—is only a click away. With all the video tutorials, courses, lecture series, and other educational offerings available online, a dedicated student might be able to acquire that 1,000 hours of knowledge significantly faster today than was possible to do in the past. But there's no getting around the fact that you'll still need to devote those 1,000 hours to learning, trying, failing, and learning some more. That is the only system for acquiring knowledge that we have ever developed.

We have a tendency to forget this. Technology has sped up so many other things that we sometimes rage at how long it takes to earn a work promotion or become an expert. A lot of us expect those things to simply *happen*, as though you can scroll through a few screens on your smartphone and suddenly have the knowledge it's taken your more-experienced colleagues a decade or two to acquire. Young People are more prone to this impatience because they were literally *born* in a world where everything has always been moving at the speed of light. But let's face it, every one of us has given up on something 15 minutes after starting because we weren't already good at it.

However, if you want to achieve success at any element of life, personal or professional, the immutable and glacial pace of advancement is a fact you absolutely *must* come to terms with. Nothing you are good at today came quickly or easily, and nothing you want to become good at will happen overnight. If you expect online dating to pair you up with the perfect match without suffering through any bad dates, you will almost certainly be disappointed. If you expect promotions at work every few months, you will have an extremely difficult time being happy at any job you ever hold. If you expect to lose 30 pounds in a month without having to exercise or change your diet or otherwise do anything disruptive, you will very likely never see the results you want. I'm currently two years into learning Spanish, and I still can't understand half of what native Spanish speakers say when they talk at their normal machine-gun rate.

Getting good at something is always a marathon; it always has been, and it always will be. If you aren't prepared to run that race, then you shouldn't expect to get any better at anything than you already are. We have done some truly awe-inspiring things, and our great-great-great-grandchildren will come up with technologies we can't even imagine. But none of that can put skills and knowledge into your head any faster than our caveman ancestors were able to do it themselves. *The Matrix* lied to us.

And that's why I hate Keanu Reeves.

How This Causes Tension

As mentioned in Chapter 4, some of the generational tensions you're experiencing at work are results of the technological revolution that separated us into two groups: people who developed their sense of self before computers and the Internet became an integral part of our daily lives and those who came after. With respect to the different attitudes Young People and Old People have about career advancement, the same forces are in effect. Today's Young People have been operating in a world where *almost* everything happens faster now than it used to. As a result, many of them have made an unfortunate but relatively honest mistake in thinking that their careers will advance more quickly than careers did in the past. After all, if everything else is moving faster now than it did before, why not this, too? Again, it's an unfortunate assumption that some of them have made, and it does fly directly in the face of all their *other* experiences—learning a sport, an instrument, a language, and so on—but there is at least a certain logic to it.

Moreover, and as we also briefly referenced in Chapter 4, many Young People have grown up watching so many stories of "overnight successes" that some of them have started to wonder why the same thing isn't happening for them. They've seen LeBron James making millions of dollars playing in the NBA before his 20th birthday; they've seen Mark Zuckerberg found a billion-dollar company in his 20s; they've seen Theo Epstein become the youngest manager of a professional baseball team at the age of 28; and every week there are hundreds or thousands of similar examples to suggest that success shouldn't be terribly difficult. Unfortunately for these Young People, what those stories almost never mention are the tens of thousands of hours of practice that James, Zuckerberg, Epstein, and all the others put into their respective careers, most of it in obscurity, until their single-minded dedication finally paid off.

Also, it would be an inexcusable omission on my part if I didn't mention that many of today's Young People have been raised in a world that has actively fostered their belief that success is easy. From scoreless soccer leagues to competitions in which all participants get a trophy to parents negotiating with teachers who give them failing grades or attempt to discipline them when they're unruly in class, we've constructed a society in which many Young People have been trained to think they don't have to work very hard to get whatever they want. Many colleges now offer luxury student housing (granite countertops, rooftop pools, free tanning, free housekeeping, etc.) that is beyond the means of many working professionals and that is all but guaranteed to disappoint students who graduate from those universities and then find that they can't live as well as an adult as they could live in school.

Plenty of books have been written about the so-called Trophy Generation, and virtually all of those books shower contempt on its entitled and misguided members. But before you do the same, try to remember who taught them what they know. Every Millennial you work with today was raised either by Baby Boomer parents or the oldest of the Gen Xers, which means that if Young People really do have a flawed understanding of the value of hard work, it's we Old People who bear some of the responsibility for the failure to teach it to them.

Advancement Never Stops

I've now explained why some of the Young People you work with think about their careers the way they do. If you're Older or more experienced than your colleagues, this should do something to bring them closer to the Us side of the line. However, the gap between Young People and Old People might still seem significant: Today's Young People are operating under the influence of different cultural and technological influences than Old People. If today's two generations are really going to find a common understanding with one another, it would be helpful if we could find some way in which both Young People and Old People behave in exactly the same way.

Fortunately for us, that's not hard to do. Because in precisely the same manner that many Young People have expressed a disinterest in putting in the time and effort to advance in their careers, plenty of Old People have expressed an identical disinterest. These people have decided that they've already learned everything they need to learn and are perfectly happy to coast as long as they can get away with it. If you don't have some Older or more-experienced colleagues who come in a few minutes late every day, leave as early as possible, consistently shoot down new ideas, and put up a fight whenever they're forced to engage in any kind of continuing education, then you almost certainly have friends in other companies or industries who have faced this problem.

It's also all but certain that if you are an Old Person, you've agreed with the vast majority of the advice for the Young People reading this. The revelation that advancement is a process surely seemed obvious to you, which we've mentioned a few times already. And this means it should be equally obvious that advancement is a process *that never stops*.

If any of your Older or more-experienced colleagues are suffering from a faulty work ethic, it's probably not that they never had one to begin with. Very few people manage to move into positions of authority, or even to survive for decades in the same position, without having worked hard to get (and stay) there. Instead, some of your Older colleagues have simply forgotten that we can never stop learning and pushing and trying new things, no matter how experienced we think we are.

This is true for both our personal and professional lives. When we addressed work ethic for Young People, we demonstrated that the process by which we improve at our careers is the same process by which we improve at sports or instruments. The same is still true whether you have 2 years' experience or 20. Concert cellists are constantly practicing in order to get even better than they already are, and 40-year-old athletes continue to train in order to stay at the top of their game. The ones who choose not to are the ones who eventually get eclipsed by their hungrier and more dedicated competitors, regardless of how old those competitors are.

In Her Own Words: Susan A. on the Importance of Staying Current

Susan A. is 53 years old and works for a global consulting firm. She admits to being frustrated with colleagues of all ages when it comes to what she views as an insufficient work ethic. Here's what she has to say about people close to her own age and experience level:

> I'm quite frankly amazed at the number of people my age who are "just getting by" and are apparently comfortable doing so. I think one of the biggest lessons I've learned in my career is that there is always something new to learn and a new way of doing things. Technology has been a big learning curve for my generation and continues to impact everything I do. I know people who are just hanging on to old ways of doing things as they near retirement. My biggest question to them is, What world are they going to live in when they leave the workforce? They have the opportunity now while they are still working to learn as much as they can—education that will carry over into their post-work life and that they aren't taking advantage of. I think it's a huge loss and mistake on their part. And it sets a terrible example for their young colleagues. How can we expect our new hires to give 110% to their jobs when they see so many people with 20+ years' experience who are doing as little as they can get away with?

Susan's story paints a vivid picture. But perhaps the best example of the true nature of advancement is the marriage example we used earlier. It would be ridiculous to propose to someone on a first date because developing healthy relationships requires a lot of time—hence, advancement is a process. However, it would be equally ridiculous to suddenly stop telling your spouse of 17 years how much you love him or her because healthy relationships require constant maintenance in order to be sustained—hence, advancement never stops.

Hopefully you see the point. Our careers require a continual effort on our part, in much the same way that our personal relationships do if we want them to be happy and successful. If you're a parent, then you've certainly had moments when you've felt like the workload was simply too much to bear—every moment a new crisis, every day another bloody nose or homework assignment or baseball practice to coach. But somehow you've found the strength to continue. Our careers require the same dogged persistence.

In many cases, those Old People who have stopped progressing in their careers have done so for two main reasons. The first, which is the simplest to explain and understand, is that they've found they can get away with it, and all of us are occasionally susceptible to doing what seems easiest. The second reason is that they believe the experience they've already accumulated should be sufficient proof of their talent and ability, and that has encouraged them toward complacency. We discuss this phenomenon in greater detail in Chapter 6, along with various ways to deal with it.

For now, what's important is that here we have a single arena in which Young People and Old People behave identically. Advancement is a process, and that process never stops. All of us have been living our entire lives according to this inevitable reality, and all of us sometimes forget the truth of it. That we sometimes forget is an issue we can work with. That we're all following the same blueprint means, once again, that we're all much more Us than Them.

The following two biographies should drive the point home. If you're struggling to instill in your Younger or less-experienced colleagues an appreciation for a robust work ethic, either of these should help you illustrate how long it sometimes takes to achieve success. If instead you're trying to convince an Older or more-experienced colleague why they shouldn't succumb to the temptation to relax, either story should reinforce the incontrovertible truth that the time to throw in the towel is exactly never.

Person Whose Work Ethic and Dedication Sort of Make Me Feel Ashamed of Myself #1

You might not know Kathryn Joosten by name, but you've probably seen her face. She was nominated for two Emmys for her role as the neighbor on *Desperate Housewives*, and she appeared in dozens of other shows, including *Seinfeld* and *Will and Grace*. She ended up doing pretty well for herself—eventually. But that wasn't always the case.

In fact, she didn't start her acting career until she was 56. After getting divorced in her 40s and hungry for a change in circumstances, Joosten spent several years failing to make a dent in the acting world, so she supported her children through a series of odd jobs that included hanging wallpaper. Eventually she landed a small part at Disney World in Orlando, but even that didn't last.

So in 1995, Joosten moved in with her son in L.A. to try and make a career out of something she had to that point completely failed to succeed at. She had no agent, no prospects, and exactly one fairly unimpressive credit on her resume.

The rest, as they say, is history.

Person Whose Work Ethic and Dedication Sort of Make Me Feel Ashamed of Myself #2

You undoubtedly know who Colonel Sanders is. Perhaps you know that the Kentucky Fried Chicken founder started his now-famous franchise when he was 65 years old. You might even know that he did it by using his first Social Security check to provide the funding for the enterprise, which has to be one of the most daring uses of Social Security in the history of that institution. But you may not know that when he chose to do so, Harland Sanders wasn't embarking on some new idea he'd been tossing around in his head for the past few years. He wasn't finally taking a gamble on an unquenchable lifelong dream. He was recovering from a series of crushing failures that had provided him all the reason in the world to never try starting another business again.

By his mid-40s, Sanders had tried a number of careers, including (according to his autobiography) working as an "amateur obstetrician," which has to be the most singularly terrifying resume item I've ever heard of. Eventually he found himself cooking food for customers at the gas station where he lived and worked. Things were going pretty well, and eventually more people were showing up for the food than for gasoline.

That is, until a new highway was built several miles away and changed all the traffic patterns. Overnight Sanders' customer base evaporated, and soon he was bankrupt. When he received his first Social Security check, he had every reason to believe he had no reason to try any harder. Better to live off a guaranteed income than risk another failure, right?

What You Can Do

As with our discussion about loyalty in Chapter 4, resolving generational differences with respect to work ethic and career advancement is much easier than it might seem. As before, the first step is to determine what Young People and Old People have in common.

Qualities, Attitudes, and Opinions That Young People and Old People Have in Common

1. All of us get better at things slowly and steadily over time. This is true for absolutely everything we do, both professionally and personally.
2. All of us, Young People as well as Old People, sometimes forget the truth of the statement above.

That's really all there is to it. Young People have a tendency to forget that advancement is a process, while Old People have a tendency to forget that the process never stops—but *everyone* is operating within the same system. As with our discussion of loyalty in the previous chapter, all of us are much more strongly Us than Them when it comes to career advancement.

Also because our careers function the way that all other experiences do, it is easy to use the example of common experiences to illustrate why slow progress and a solid work ethic are essential for career advancement at every stage of a person's career. One of the most effective ways to convince anyone of anything is to use examples that relate directly to their own lives, and we discuss this in more detail shortly, when we talk about strategies.

Now for step two—explaining why the people from each generation think and behave the way they do. Obviously, we've just spent most of the chapter looking at this in detail, but the following summaries should convince you that these differences are actually quite small and, more importantly, eminently manageable.

Key Concepts: Why Your Younger or Less-Experienced Colleagues Think and Behave the Way They Do

1. Many Young People mistakenly believe that because technology has accelerated virtually everything we do, it must necessarily accelerate the pace at which we acquire skills and knowledge. This can be easily corrected by pointing to the process by which they themselves have developed proficiency in anything they consider themselves to be proficient at.

2. Some Young People are more experienced than their age would suggest and expect to be judged based on that experience.

3. Some Young People simply do not have a strong work ethic, either because they are naturally lazy or because they have been raised in a culture that rewarded them regardless of their ability or effort.

Key Concepts: Why Your Older or More-Experienced Colleagues Think and Behave the Way They Do

1. Old People have been going through the process of advancement longer than Young People, and for that reason, they expect to be respected for the work they have done up to this point.

2. Some Old People no longer have the solid work ethic that has carried them from the beginning of their careers until now, either because they've become complacent or because they believe they can skate by with minimal repercussions.

Again, you'll notice significant similarities here. Some Young People are naturally lazy, and some Old People have become lazy. Anyone who has a certain amount of experience, whether a Young Person or an Old Person, expects to be respected for that experience.

So if you are a Young Person and want to have a decent working relationship with your Older or more-experienced colleagues, make sure they know that you respect their experience. You can accomplish this in a number of ways but probably most easily by simply consulting them to learn from them the strategies they have traditionally found to be successful. And if your Older colleagues seem to be constantly demanding that you work harder than you currently are, try to recognize that insistence for what it is—that they've been around long enough to see the rewards of their own hard work, and they want the same for you.

In Her Own Words: Dr. Eva R. on What Her Boss Taught Her

Dr. Eva R. is 29 years old and works as a chemist for a multinational chemical company. In her own words:

I spent five and a half years in grad school earning my PhD, and I honestly felt that once I had successfully defended my thesis, I was "done." It was such an exhausting process, and I felt like I had earned the world's respect. So when I started my job, it was enormously demoralizing to realize that I was once again the lowest person on the totem pole. I felt like I had just climbed a mountain only to find another, taller one right in front of me, and in the first few months of my job, I wasn't sure I had the strength to keep pushing.

Thankfully, one of my bosses was astute enough to realize what I was going through. He'd been with the company for over 20 years and had seen dozens of newly minted PhDs struggle to adjust to their new careers. He spent hours talking with me about his own career path, and while he empathized with my frustration, he also made it clear that there would never be a time in my life when I could just sit back and coast. At some level, I already knew the truth of what he was telling

> me, but having a boss who really seemed to understand what I was going through meant a lot to me. I definitely have a better appreciation for how my career is going to progress as a result of all our conversations.

Whether you like it or not, Young People, your Older or more-experienced colleagues are the gatekeepers for your company. It's a position they worked their way into, just as you will someday work your way into it, and it's a position that comes with an enormous amount of influence. They know how to get things done. They know who you need to talk to. They know which rules you need to follow religiously and which ones you can afford to bend a little bit. You need to treat your Older colleagues like the assets they are instead of looking at them as obstacles you have to figure out how to avoid or overcome. Remember from our conversation about loyalty, it is primarily the responsibility of the Older or more-experienced generation to begin the conversation and create the right conditions for developing a culture in which loyalty can thrive. Here, however, it's Young People who need to begin the conversation. Your Older or more-experienced colleagues have earned it.

However, if you're Older or more experienced than the people you're trying to work with, you aren't totally off the hook here. It's *your* job to recognize that respect when it's given and respond by helping your Younger or less-experienced colleagues along the path to their own career advancement. Several people—coaches, colleagues, great managers, and others—have helped you reach the level you're at today, and really the *only* way that a business survives past its founders is for its more-experienced employees to coach and train the less-experienced ones. That is the essence of succession planning.

Also, remember the Sun Microsystems mentorship study from the previous chapter? Choosing to mentor one of your promising Younger colleagues will end up being as beneficial for your own career as it will be for the person you mentor. So you can reach out to your promising younger colleagues because it's the right thing to do for them and for your business, or you can do it because it will help you personally. You win either way.

In His Own Words: Tyler H. on the Power of Mentoring

Tyler H. is 42 years old and owns a small marketing and web design company. In his own words:

I started my career working for a large marketing company that downsized and cut my position in 2006, so I decided to take my skills and start my own business. For years I worked by myself out of my home, and I was making a decent but not spectacular living. By 2012 I realized that I needed some part-time assistance, so I hired Kiley to help me 20 hours a week. She was 22 and hadn't been able to find a full-time job after graduating from college. I fully expected her to leave in a few months once she found something more stable, and that was fine with me because I wasn't sure that I'd need her for more than a few months.

However, from the very beginning, Kiley demonstrated a desire to learn everything about my business. We would agree to meet at coffee shops to work for a couple hours, but she would often stay longer than we had planned—and without being paid for her time—so she could ask questions and bounce ideas off me. Sometimes she would send emails or leave unasked-for voicemails with new strategies she had thought up. She never seemed to mind that I was "just" a one-person business. I was paying her to handle some of the "grunt work," but I soon found that I really enjoyed having someone to strategize with. Because of our conversations, I started thinking about things I might never have been confident enough to consider on my own—renting office space, taking out a business loan, paying for advertising, growing my business. I guess I'd always assumed that my business would die whenever I decided to quit, but here was this ambitious 22-year-old helping me realize that maybe it didn't have to be that way. Maybe I could actually create something sustainable and bigger than myself.

I eventually hired Kiley full time, along with two other part-time employees. We currently work out of a co-working space, and 2014 was our best year ever. I don't know what's ultimately going to happen, but I know I have Kiley to thank for it.

Also, it's important to point out that work ethic and loyalty are related qualities. If you're struggling with a Young or inexperienced employee who doesn't seem to have the kind of work ethic you expect—or even an Older colleague who seems to have lost interest in working as hard as before—make sure you're doing everything you can to create the right environment to encourage their best efforts. Try also to remember that while there may not be anything you can do to correct years of bad training, you can easily address any unreasonable expectations your colleagues of all ages might have about the speed at which their careers will advance.

But enough philosophizing. Let's get to the strategies. As before, regardless of which side of the generational divide you find yourself on, the things you need to do here won't cost you a dime.

Strategies for Addressing Issues of Career Advancement or Work Ethic

- **Find an Older or more-experienced person in your department or company and ask him or her to be your mentor.** Don't just assume the person will help you; specifically ask him or her to do so, and say that you're asking because you respect the person and want to learn how to achieve what he or she has achieved. This won't work 100% of the time, as some of your Older or more-experienced peers will be legitimately too busy or will have promised their mentoring time to others, but it will eventually work if you ask enough people. Asking will not come off as idle flattery if you're sincere; and since you can't fake sincerity, your first step is to recognize that your Older or more-experienced colleagues have done some fairly impressive things in their careers. Most of us are happy to help others, but all of us want to feel as though the people we're helping appreciate that we're doing so. If you make them feel appreciated, they'll return the favor by teaching you what they've learned—and trust me, that will save you a *ton* of time.

- **If you have some Young colleagues or employees with substandard work ethics, compare their careers to other common experiences they may be familiar with.** As I said before, the examples of learning an instrument or playing a sport are great metaphors for discussing career advancement. Almost everyone has tried to learn an instrument, play a sport, or learn a second language. Those who have found success will remember that they only achieved that success through hard work and years of dedication; and those who quit will realize that it's impossible to get better at something without practicing it. This won't create a killer work ethic in someone (more on that later), but it will at least put into perspective the nature of the working world.

- **Share your own path to professional success with your Young colleagues or employees.** I'd be willing to bet that most of your Younger or less-experienced colleagues have no idea how long it took you to get where you are today—and you can't blame them for not knowing if you've never told them. If you didn't get your first promotion for four years, make sure your new hires know it, and then tell them exactly what you did in order to make it happen. As we discussed in the previous chapter, Young People simply want to know that their hard work is going to be rewarded. If you can show them a blueprint for success *and* that it's one they can repeat for themselves, they'll be far more inclined to put in the effort.

- **If you are Younger or more inexperienced than most of your colleagues, make it clear that you are prepared to work hard.** Unfortunately for you, many Old People are justifiably skeptical of the work ethic of today's Young People. (This is a constant dynamic of Old/Young relations, by the way, and is not unique to today's working culture. The Greatest Generation also thought that their Baby Boomer children weren't terribly interested in hard work, and there were plenty of long-haired hippies lying around to prove that to them.) Probably the best way to alleviate their suspicions is to say, clearly and unambiguously, that you are willing to work hard for your career. Doing so is not the same as promising to work 150 hours every week until you're miserable and nearly dead from exhaustion. You'll have to determine for yourself what the proper balance is between your job and the rest of your life. But simply stating your intention to work hard will set you apart from those who either don't plan to do so or who simply assume that their superiors will eventually figure out for themselves how dedicated they are.

- **Instill an appreciation for delayed gratification by presenting the impending retirement of your Older workers as an opportunity for your Younger workers.** This is an interesting tactic that doesn't get enough attention. According to the Pew Research Center, approximately 10,000 Baby Boomers will be turning 65 *every day for the next 16 years*. Many companies are expecting significant percentages of their workforce to retire in the next decade. I've seen this personally as I've delivered keynote addresses and training sessions for hundreds of different companies. Companies everywhere are facing a shortage of skilled workers ready and able to replace those who are about to retire. If your company or department is one of them, you can spin this as an excellent reason for your Youngest or least-experienced workers to settle in for the long haul. For example, if you're trying to encourage a 26-year-old entry-level employee to dedicate more time and energy to her job, point out that a decade from now, she'll be one of the most senior people in her department. At 36 years old, she'll be in a position she might otherwise not have been able to expect until her mid-40s, all because your company's demographics are playing in her favor—provided, of course, that she's willing to do the work.

- **Periodically highlight examples of people who succeeded after repeated failures or other setbacks.** Older or more-experienced workers have a tendency to think they've learned everything they need to or that they've reached a point where they can "get by" without having to exert themselves. One of the easiest ways for you to combat this tendency is to repeatedly share success stories of people who refused to settle into that kind of destructive inertia. This could be about anything from a valuable lesson you learned at the most recent conference you attended to a colleague who finally secured a major contract with a high-value customer after several failed attempts to do so. The more often you can highlight the value of perseverance, the more likely others will follow that example.

- **Emphasize the similarities between professional and personal success.** Most of your colleagues, regardless of their age or experience level, will have either been married or spent some amount of time in a serious relationship. Many of them will have children. And all of them have been sons, daughters, brothers, sisters, or friends. In all of our personal relationships, we instinctively realize that we occasionally have to exert a certain amount of effort in order to make the relationship work. We all know that we can't afford to take our marriages for granted if we want them to thrive. And those same qualities are true of our professional lives as well. If you can make your colleagues connect their ideal behavior in their personal lives with their ideal behavior at work, you'll help them realize that what you're asking really isn't any different than what they've been doing their entire lives.

- **Point out, when applicable, that age and experience are not *always* correlated.** It is usually true that Older people have more experience than Younger ones. The only way we get good at things is by working at them over time. However, it is not always true that a 50-year-old has more experience than a 25-year-old. Nowhere is this more obviously true than in the world of computer programming, where it's frequently the case that people become 10,000-hour experts while still in their teens. If you operate in an industry where your people might have received some amount of training before they become official employees, do what you can to encourage others to take that training into consideration. Sometimes the youngest member of your team starts at a much higher level than you might expect because he or she has spent a few years tinkering with machines in the garage—and if that's the case, make sure your Older employees are aware of it. (This will be enormously easier if you couple this with the suggestion in Chapter 4 of inviting your Young People to deliver presentations on topics they already know something about.) If it's true that Old People deserve respect for the experience they've worked so hard to acquire, it's equally true for any Young People who have done the same.

- **When necessary, fire your Young employees quickly or encourage your Older ones into early retirement.** You cannot create a work ethic in somebody. You can show people the importance of working hard, and you can provide a variety of economic and psychological benefits to reward people for their effort; we've already discussed how you can do those things. But you can't invent a work ethic in someone who has decided that working hard just isn't their thing, and there are plenty of those people at every age and experience level. Some never had a strong work ethic to begin with, and others have decided to do only as much as is necessary to continue collecting a paycheck. Neither approach is a healthy one, and neither should be tolerated.

So if you have a Young employee who doesn't seem interested in working hard, and you've tried everything we've already discussed—you've provided mentoring opportunities, you've given the person strong reasons to be excited about what you're offering in terms of job security and potential, you've explained how career advancement works, and you've made comparisons between professional excellence and proficiency in sports and instruments and other common experiences—if you've done *everything* you can think to do and they still won't work hard, then get rid of them as quickly as you're able. They've made a decision not to give you what you need from them, and you shouldn't waste any more time trying to work with someone who isn't interested in working with you.

And if your Older or more-experienced colleagues have decided to stop pushing themselves and have given you every indication that they plan to simply stagnate or backslide until they can sneak quietly away into retirement, they deserve the same treatment. Their years of service and previous dedication will probably earn them a little more leniency than you would give to a newly hired employee, but eventually a determined disinterest in working hard should earn everyone the same result, regardless of their age or experience level.

Fundamentally, the generational issue over career advancement boils down to a simple fact that we've already mentioned but that bears repeating: All of us, regardless of our age and experience, occasionally forget something we're supposed to remember. Young People often forget that getting older is the *only* way that we are able to gain experience and advance, and Old People often forget that our careers are rarely static, just as our personal lives aren't. You'll notice that these strategies are largely a combination of providing reminders, examples, or new perspectives. These are all fairly simple concepts to understand. As we've pointed out over and over again, resolving your generational issues in the workplace isn't complicated.

Nowhere will that simplicity be more obvious than in the next chapter. One of the most consistent complaints Young People have about their Older or more-experienced colleagues is that they only want to do things the way they've always done them. There's an absurdly easy explanation for why Old People think the way they do, and we examine it shortly. We'll also talk about why that isn't always a failsafe strategy for success. But mostly we explain why Old People aren't quite as stubborn and terrified as they're often made out to be.

So what are you waiting for? You're almost done with this book, which means you're almost done figuring out how to resolve every generational issue you will ever face in the workplace. I know you'd rather be jet skiing or whittling or whatever it is you like to do in your spare time, but don't you think solving all your problems is worth a little delayed gratification? (See what I did there? Hurray for callbacks!) So turn the page already!

Key Strategies for Resolving Issues with Your Younger or Less-Experienced Colleagues

(Reproduced from Chapter 4)

1. Present your new hires with business cards on their first day of work.

2. Invite your newest employees or team members to deliver a presentation to the rest of your team on a topic they already know something about.

3. Learn their names quickly, call them by name when you say hello, and praise them as often as you can think to.

4. If you are in a supervisory role, tell everyone who directly reports to you that you will go to bat for them if necessary.

5. Solicit the opinions of everyone who directly reports to you on a regular basis.

6. Invite your colleagues and employees to lunch on a weekly or monthly basis.

7. If you are a supervisor or manager, ask them what they want out of their jobs *over and above* the salary and benefits your company provides.

8. Offer your services as a mentor or create a mentorship program.

9. Give them the opportunity to use their skills and abilities on a regular basis.

(Chapter 5)

10. **If you have some Young colleagues or employees with substandard work ethics, compare their careers to other common experiences they may be familiar with.**

11. **Share your own path to professional success with your Young colleagues or employees.**

12. **Instill an appreciation for delayed gratification by presenting the impending retirement of your Older workers as an opportunity for your Younger workers.**

13. **Periodically highlight examples of people who succeeded after repeated failures or other setbacks.**

14. **Emphasize the similarities between professional and personal successes.**

15. **Point out, when applicable, that age and experience are not always correlated.**

16. **If necessary, fire your Young employees quickly.**

Key Strategies for Resolving Issues with Your Older or More-Experienced Colleagues

(Reproduced from Chapter 4)

1. If you are in a supervisory role, tell everyone who directly reports to you that you will go to bat for them if necessary.

2. Solicit the opinions of everyone who directly reports to you on a regular basis.

3. Invite your colleagues and employees to lunch on a weekly or monthly basis.

4. Ask your colleagues and employees why they have stayed with your company as long as they have.

5. If you are a supervisor or manager, ask your colleagues and employees what they want out of their jobs *over and above* the salary and benefits your company provides.

6. Give your colleagues and employees the opportunity to use their skills and abilities on a regular basis.

7. Tell your manager or other senior employees that you intend to spend your career working your way up the ladder at your company.

(Chapter 5)

8. **Find an Older or more-experienced person and ask him or her to be your mentor.**

9. **If you are Younger or more inexperienced than most of your colleagues, make it clear that you are prepared to work hard.**

10. **Periodically highlight examples of people who succeeded after repeated failures or other setbacks.**

11. **Emphasize the similarities between professional and personal success.**

12. **Point out, when applicable, that age and experience are not *always* correlated.**

13. **If necessary, encourage your Older employees into early retirement.**

6

On the Tension Between Stasis and Innovation

You now know why some of your colleagues do not immediately display a deep sense of company loyalty. You know why some of them don't come into their professional lives with a killer work ethic. You know why some of them have erroneous expectations about how quickly their careers will advance and about how hard they'll need to work in order to maintain their professional edge. You know why some of them have started to work less vigorously than they did in the past. And, most importantly, you know how to address all of these issues—how to instill loyalty in everyone around you, how to encourage your Younger or less-experienced colleagues to work hard and how to remind your Older or more-experienced colleagues that they shouldn't stop working hard. At this point, the vast majority of your generational issues in the workplace could probably be resolved.[1]

In fact, there's really only one major area of generational tension left, and that is the nature and pace of change. Typically, Young People expect changes to happen more often and more quickly than Old People do. If you're experiencing generational tensions related to changing elements of your business, then it's almost certainly because some of your Older colleagues don't see the point in changing *anything*, while some of your Younger colleagues seem determined to change *everything*. Old People tend to say, "Love it or leave it," while Young

---

[1] Presuming, of course, that your colleagues are actually willing to listen to you. That's a big *if* since you probably wouldn't have any generational issues in the first place if everyone were happy to listen to the ideas and advice of people 20 years older or younger than they are. But fear not! You'll find solutions to that problem in Chapters 9–10. Hurray for Chapters 9–10!

People tend to say, "Love it or change it." Our differing approaches to change are one of the foundational causes of generational issues. When we disagree with someone about how much or how quickly to change something, we immediately move farther away from that person on the Us/Them spectrum.

In Her Own Words: Alison J. on Staying the Course

Alison J. is 51 years old and works for the corporate headquarters of a major clothing retailer. Among other things, she is in charge of giving store tours to new employees so they can better understand the front end of their business. In her own words:

> I've given hundreds of store tours at this point, and I can already tell you what they're going to say. Most of our new people have just received their MBAs or have a financial background. They're numbers people. So they always say we should reduce the size of the dressing rooms in order to fit more of them into each store; that way, we can handle more customers per hour and make more money. They all say that. It used to irritate me to no end. They think they know so much more than I do, but they have no concept of the idea that we're trying to create an experience, and that experience requires us to make sure that our customers feel pampered and luxurious. Now it just amuses me. I always listen to their comments and pretend like I haven't heard them a thousand times already. They'll learn eventually. They always do.

In His Own Words: Alan S. on The Problem with 'Business as Usual'

We first met Alan S. in Chapter 2. He's the 36-year-old Gen Xer working for a startup marketing firm. It turns out that he had some issues with the way his older colleagues approached new ideas. In his own words:

> I was 23 when I started working for my company. I bought in to the promise of huge potential and getting in on the ground floor and all that. And the company really did have

great potential to be successful, but it definitely lacked when it came to sales and execution. Regarding idea generation, I think the problem was that the executives were making decisions based on what used to work for them in the past. This was a new company with a new type of product. Now that in itself should let you know that the older executives who started the company were capable of good ideas, but they were using "what worked in the past" techniques to try and sell our products, and it simply didn't work. I didn't have any history or experience to confuse me, so my ideas for improvement were strictly based on what I thought would work. That's not to say you don't learn and improve from experience—you do— but experienced people have been constantly fine-tuning and simplifying "what works," so they are sometimes less likely to take a big risk or think too far outside their norm. Sometimes being new and green can allow you to come up with ideas that an experienced person wouldn't, maybe because a young person's processes aren't so fine-tuned yet.

Ultimately, we continued doing things the way the older executives wanted to do them, it continued to be unsuccessful, and our startup eventually went out of business. I'm not saying things would necessarily have been different if they'd been more willing to listen to my ideas or get out of their comfort zone because I can't know that for certain. But it certainly couldn't have been any worse.

You'll notice that these two stories are very similar to the ones at the beginning of Chapter 5. In both chapters, an Old Person is complaining about a Young Person's chronic impatience and unwillingness to learn the ropes before voicing unreasonable expectations; and in both cases, a Young Person is complaining about Old People's stubborn refusal to push out their comfort zones. In a way it makes sense that these two issues would be related because the very nature of career advancement involves a continual change from beginner to expert.

We're going to divide the subject of change management into two parts. Chapter 7 will deal more specifically with how to discuss changes to your business when they become inevitable and how to integrate those changes in a way that will maximize consensus and minimize dissent, regardless of your people's age or experience level.

In this chapter, however, we're going to discuss why different generations tend to have different attitudes toward change and innovation in the first place. Why is it that so many of your Older colleagues seem to be perfectly content to keep doing things the way they've always done them? And why is it that so many of your Younger colleagues seem to be constantly agitating for more and more innovation when it doesn't always seem to be necessary?

We'll find out shortly. But first, I think it's time for another quiz.

The Reason Old People Like Doing Things the Way They've Always Done Them...

I know, I know—books like this are supposed to be passively read. Or maybe you're only halfway listening to this in your car while you curse at other drivers. The point is, you're not supposed to have to actually *do* anything. But this quiz only has two questions, so I think you'll survive.

1. If you would like to propose to a woman, which of the following should you probably buy her as a symbol of your eternal love and devotion?

    A. A diamond ring

    B. A Shetland pony

    C. An arc welder

    D. Paint

2. If you would like the undivided attention of one of your customers, which of the following is the best way to get it?

    A. Call the customer.

    B. Send the customer a text.

    C. Send the customer an email message.

    D. Send the customer a message through social media.

As with the quiz in Chapter 3, you are free to answer however you wish. And there are technically no wrong answers. It's possible that you married a welder's daughter, or maybe you're the kind of woman who has always wanted to sculpt giant steel lawn ornaments, in which case the arc welder probably sounds like a great idea. Paint is always nice. And personally, I think half of the married women in the world would have said yes to their husbands if those men had proposed with a pony. If you happen to be thinking about proposing to someone in the near future, keep it in mind. Walk up to the woman of your dreams with a Shetland pony in tow and say, "He'll be yours if you'll be mine." Women love ponies; I've known that since I was a kid. It very well might work.

But of course I already know how you answered Question 1 because everyone answers it the same. Thousands of years have trained us to know that the diamond ring is *the* symbol of an engagement. When you buy a diamond ring and get down on one knee, you're not being original. You're not being innovative. You're not doing something completely unexpected. You're not going against the grain or blazing a new trail or whatever maverick-y metaphor you're using right now. You're following a well-established tradition, and you're doing it because you know that it works.

The same is true for Question 2, for which you almost certainly answered A as well. Calling someone on the phone isn't a novel solution. When you make a phone call, you're not taking advantage of a disruptive technology or changing an established paradigm in favor of something newer and better. You're doing what people have been doing for the past 100 years, and you're doing it because out of all the options I gave you, calling someone on the phone is the only one that might earn you their undivided attention. You might not always choose to make a phone call; after all, sending a text or an email is certainly an easier and less time-consuming way to touch base with someone, and sometimes that's all you're trying to do. But if you want to make sure they're paying attention to you and nobody else, texts and emails simply can't beat a good, old-fashioned phone call.

What's the point of this quiz? Well, if you happen to be a Young Person, these two questions illustrate the most critical piece of information you need to understand in order to appreciate why your Older or more-experienced colleagues are occasionally resistant to innovation in general and your suggestions in particular. In fact, *resistant* isn't even the right word to be using because they're not actually resisting anything. A lot of times they simply don't see the purpose of changing the way they're doing things.

Why? Because the way they've always done things them *has generally worked.*

This is actually so important that it bears repeating, and in larger type!

The reason many Older or more-experienced people like doing things the way they've always done them is that the way they've always done them has generally worked.

Shocking as this may be, your Older or more-experienced colleagues actually do know what they're doing. They know what they're doing so well, in fact, that they were able to create a company profitable and sustainable enough to need to hire Young People like you in order to keep things going. If your team or department or company is currently successful, then that success is the result of current practices and processes. I realize this might be a difficult pill to swallow, especially if you're of the mindset that certain changes need to occur soon in order for you to stay competitive. It's very possible that you're correct, and we address those concerns in a few pages.

But for now, it's essential to understand that whatever practices and processes your company is currently doing are the best and most highly evolved practices and processes that anyone who has ever worked there has ever been able to come up with. It's not simply that whatever you're doing right now works; it's that it works better than anything else that has ever been tried. That doesn't mean those practices and processes can't be improved, and we talk about that shortly. But it *does* mean that they have been successful up to this point.

In fact, look at the top 10 companies in the Fortune 500 for 2014: Wal-Mart, Exxon, Chevron, Berkshire Hathaway, Apple, Phillips 66, General Motors, Ford Motor, General Electric, and Valero Energy. None of these companies achieved its market dominance because of its vibrant social media presence. Many of them are selling substantially the same products and services they were selling a decade ago.

With the exception of Apple, none of them generates the majority of its income by bringing disruptive products to the consumer market. By and large, these are not the companies whose flashy CEOs and sexy gadgets monopolize the attention of business columnists and tech bloggers. Some of their employees still use cathode-ray monitors and dot-matrix printers, just like cavepeople used to. And yet every one of these companies is wildly successful. I'm not suggesting that Wal-Mart or Exxon or any of the others don't care about innovation; they absolutely do. But they certainly don't care about *every* innovation or about innovation for its own sake.

If you want to see a concrete example of a successful company that has absolutely no interest in innovation for innovation's sake, look no further than the Berkshire Hathaway homepage (www.berkshire-hathaway.com). It is, without a doubt, the crappiest homepage I have ever seen. It's conceivable that Warren Buffett designed it on a napkin while he was bored on a conference call. In fact, it's possible that the Berkshire Hathaway homepage actually predates the Internet because there's absolutely no way this page has been updated since 1843. The Berkshire Hathaway homepage is the technological equivalent of a giant, steaming turd. That's how bad it is. And if I ever meet Warren Buffett in person, I'll say the same to his face.

And if I ever do have the opportunity to speak at the Berkshire Hathaway annual shareholders' meeting in Omaha and say what I've just written while Warren Buffett is in attendance, here's how I imagine he might reply.

> *Thanks for your comments, Jeff. I appreciate your efforts to help us improve our branding and the user experience for our online customers. Except wait—oh, that's right, we're not a consumer company, and we have never been. We don't get business because some giant conglomerate spent a few minutes browsing through our website. So ultimately, the quality of our homepage doesn't really matter. Besides, I think we've done a pretty good job of branding ourselves, and I'm worth $50 billion. So thanks for your thoughts, and go away.*

Again, I'm not suggesting that Warren Buffett is disinterested in innovation. Obviously, he's always looking for new, interesting, innovative ways to make money. Exxon and Chevron are always looking for new and innovative ways to find oil. Ford and General Motors are always developing new engines and car designs. Wal-Mart and Apple are always experimenting with their store layouts and product placement in order to increase sales. At every point in time for every business, the drive to innovate is paramount, and the most successful companies are the ones that do it better than their competitors.

So while Young People have a tendency to criticize their Older colleagues for being unwilling to innovate, that complaint isn't very valid. Everyone, regardless of age or experience, appreciates the need to innovate. The question is rarely *whether* to innovate. Far more commonly, the question is *how* to innovate. The only people you work with who don't appreciate the necessity of innovation are people who don't feel like putting in the energy that will be required of them to learn whatever new skills innovations will demand. This happens among Young People and Old People alike—the lazy new employ-ees and the retired-in-all-but-name veterans—and in Chapter 5 we already discussed what you should do with those people.

However, while every motivated professional understands the importance of innovation, Older People have a much deeper appre-ciation of the value of existing practices and processes, if for no other reason than that they've been around long enough to see the ben-efits of those systems.[2] If you're a Young Person, it's important for you to understand that your Older or more-experienced colleagues don't have a problem with new ideas. They've been incorporating new ideas into their working model for their entire careers. What they *do* have a problem with is any implication that their current practices and processes aren't successful when the reality of your business says otherwise. If your business is doing well, then it is precisely because of all those old, boring, unoriginal, stodgy, pedestrian things your col-leagues have been doing for the past few years.

You've almost certainly heard a colleague complain about a pro-posed change with the change-averse mantra of the resistant Luddite: "That's not how we've always done things." But if you unpack that statement, you'll find that in many cases, the person uttering those

---

[2] They've also been around long enough to see some of the deficiencies of those systems, which is why the call for innovation comes as often from them as it does from your Younger or less-experienced colleagues.

words isn't afraid of change. He's not necessarily saying, "That's not how we've always done things, so I refuse to consider doing them differently." A lot of times he's saying, "That's not how we've always done things, and I haven't noticed any major problems, *so why am I being asked to change something that seems to be working just fine?*" Like everyone, this person wants to know *why* he's being asked to consider a new idea. If you can't provide a compelling argument for the need to innovate, then it's very possible that the "innovation" you're touting isn't as critical or promising as you'd like it to be.

In fact, because "that's not how we've always done things" is just as often uttered out of confusion as it is out of stubborn and irrational recalcitrance, the only time you shouldn't pay it any attention is when the practice or process in question is obviously failing. If your department or company is floundering or in imminent danger of dissolution, then absolutely nothing should be sacred. In this kind of crisis, a complete overhaul might be your only chance to avoid a total collapse. Indeed, this is exactly the kind of behavior we see when new executives take over struggling companies—for example, Yahoo!'s Marissa Mayer changing flex-time policies for employees or BlackBerry's John Chen suggesting that BlackBerry might soon transition out of the phone-making business altogether in order to focus on software and other managed services. When it's an issue of survival, the consideration normally reserved for "business as usual" goes right out the window.

However, we're usually not talking about life-or-death scenarios; more commonly we're talking about isolated initiatives that may or may not be improvements to the way you're currently doing things. The only way to find out if your new marketing strategy or factory floor layout actually makes things better is to get it implemented, and the only way that's going to happen is if you can get buy-in from the other people you work with. If you're positioning your ideas as a cure-all for your company's backward approach to its logistics support or CRM strategy or whatever the issue happens to be, you'll probably experience significant pushback from your more-experienced colleagues because they'll feel that you don't value what they've accomplished so far; this is the natural reaction all of us have when we feel as though our contributions aren't being valued. If, however, you frame your innovative solution as an improvement to your currently successful practices, you'll be far more likely to get the support you need to see your innovation through.

Fundamentally, your Older or more-experienced colleagues are asking for respect—not only for themselves personally, which we discussed in Chapter 5, but also for the systems and strategies they've spent their professional lives developing and executing. They value innovation, but they also see no reason to summarily throw out the baby with the bathwater.[3]

So Why Are Young People So Eager to Change All the Time?

We've now firmly established the value of existing practices and processes. All around the world, Old People are rejoicing. "Finally, someone who understands!" If you're an Old Person yourself, you should be pleased that I've just stuck it to all the Young People reading this book.[4]

And yet I'm certain you're at least subconsciously aware that the earlier use of the phrase "business as usual" was a convenient and completely inaccurate way to describe business of any kind. All of us are constantly incorporating changes into our businesses all the time. I'd bet everything I have—and I have a lot of things that I'm fond of and don't want to give you—that you're not doing business in the same way as you were two years ago. You're using new technologies or operating under new budgets; you're dealing with new regulations and different customer demands; you've hired some new people and watched some old friends retire; and if none of that is true, you have spent the past two years quietly evolving your relationships with the colleagues, customers, and vendors that allow your business to survive and thrive. You already know this. You're constantly aware of the fact

---

[3] And since we're on the subject, just don't throw babies at all. People don't like it, and I'm pretty sure it's illegal. So don't throw babies. That's a big takeaway from this book.

[4] You've also conveniently forgotten (like all of us tend to) that you railed against the status quo when you were young just as much as today's Young People do. But I see no need to bring that up.

that things are always changing and that you're always being forced to adapt to those changes.

So if it's true that we're all always incorporating changes into our existing working model—and it *is* true—then why does it seem like today's Young People are so much more impatient for change than their Older colleagues?

There are three reasons for it. The first is simple enough to understand and easy enough to forget if you're no longer at the beginning of your career: Advocating for change is one of the most common tools Young People use to demonstrate their own intelligence and earn the respect of their Older or more-experienced peers. As we mature, all of us yearn to be taken seriously by our elders, and one of the best weapons we have at our disposal is to offer up ideas, solutions, strategies, and philosophies that cause our elders to pause, consider, and ultimately realize that we deserve their time and attention. This is a function of age, pure and simple, and it has been going on throughout recorded history and will continue for as long as human beings exist.

So on the one hand, Young People agitate for change because that's one of the ways Young People throughout history have always tried to be heard. Second—and more immediately relevant to your particular circumstances—the world is changing faster now than it used to. You've heard this before, probably so many times by now that your eyes are starting to roll back into your head. By itself it's a useless comment, the kind of bland throwaway sentence people sometimes use to half-heartedly justify their desire to do something different. It's said so often that it's easy to wonder if it's actually true. I've heard a million times in my life that reading in the dark is bad for your eyes, and it turns out there's no definitive proof of that. So is the "things are changing faster now than they used to" argument the same kind of misguided conventional wisdom?

Unfortunately, no. Things actually *are* changing more quickly now than in the past, and here's a brief example. In the 30 years between 1950 and 1980, our communication strategies changed absolutely not at all. If you wanted to talk to someone who was not physically in the room with you, you could either write them a letter or call them on a landline phone. Those were your only two options. For three decades, nothing changed.

However, the 30 years between 1980 and 2010 are a different story. It's difficult to pin down exactly how many new methods of communication have popped up in the past three decades, but here's a sampling:

- Mobile phones
- Email
- PDAs with a stylus and modified alphabet (remember that one?)
- Text messaging
- Video chat
- Instant messaging
- Virtual conferencing

I've probably missed a few. The point is, in the 30 years between 1980 and 2010, we added several new methods of communication into our existing portfolio. That might not seem like a lot, but it's infinitely more than we came up with between 1950 and 1980.

Perhaps this will put things into a clearer perspective. Match. com, which upended thousands of years of established courtship practices by allowing people who might otherwise never meet to find each other through the Internet, launched in 1995; here we are, 20 years later, and more than one-third of all marriages start online. Netflix, which introduced mail-order DVDs and basically destroyed the brick-and-mortar movie rental business,[5] was founded in 1997; barely 15 years later, half of all U.S. homes subscribed to Netflix, Hulu Plus, Amazon Prime, or another video streaming service. TiVo, which revolutionized the way we watch television and completely changed the advertising world's revenue models, was founded in 1999; just over a decade later, in 2012, over half of all U.S. homes were using DVRs. iTunes, which forever transformed the music industry, debuted in 2001; in 2013, digital music revenue accounted for 39% of the music industry's total global revenue. YouTube, which has given everyone with a camera the ability to become actor, director, teacher, reporter, expert, and critic, opened its digital doors in 2005; two years later, in

---

[5] Except for Family Video, whose growth and success in a decaying industry could make a business book all by itself.

2007, it consumed as much bandwidth as *the entire Internet in 2000*, and it is now the world's second-largest search engine.

As you can see, each of these innovations has fundamentally altered an industry landscape in less than 20 years. By comparison, the first gasoline-powered automobile debuted in 1886, and 20 years later fewer than 8% of U.S. households had one. The television was developed as the combination of a series of technologies in the 1920s; by 1948, a mere 0.4% of U.S. households had one. So yes, things are changing faster now than they used to.

But again, that's an overused and unhelpful platitude. So let's change the phrasing a bit.

If you're an Old Person—that is, if you came to maturity before the Internet really took hold, which we discussed in greater detail in Chapter 4—then for you today's world is changing *faster than it used to*. The pace of change has accelerated, as have the number of changes that impose themselves on a daily or weekly or monthly basis relative to what you experienced when you were younger.

However, if you're a Young Person—if you came to maturity after the Internet really took hold—then today's world is changing for you *at exactly the same speed that it always has*.

This is the critical distinction. Today's Young People are moving at the only speed they've ever known. This rapid-fire world is the only one they've ever lived in. This is their normal, and more importantly for our purposes, that's why they like it.

When we talk about different attitudes toward change, the rise of the Internet has split us into two generations as neatly as a surgical knife. That's not to say all Old People move slowly or that all Young People can't stay focused. But it does mean that Old People have almost universally been forced to *adapt* to today's hyperactive world, while Young People were almost universally *born* in it, and that distinction has led to some difficulty. Many Old People want the world to move at the speed that it used to and so occasionally respond to new ideas with kneejerk dismissal, while many Young People have little experience with or appreciation for established best practices because they're accustomed to seeing "best practices" replaced every 18 months.

Our different perceptions about the speed at which the modern world is changing is probably the most significant factor in explaining why Young People and Old People often approach change from different angles. Very simply, these two generations have grown up with markedly different expectations about the speed at which changes will and should occur. So if you are a Young Person frustrated by the apparent resistance of an Older colleague to a new idea or innovation, try to appreciate that some of that person's resistance might be due to the fact that she is struggling to come to terms with how frequently she's being asked to change. And if you're an Old Person trying to persuade a Younger colleague to operate at a more rational pace, keep in mind that she might be agitating for constant change because she's been trained to believe that she will otherwise be left behind by a world she's never seen move slowly.

There is a third factor at play as well, and it has to do with one of the most dangerous words in the business world: *complacency*.

The Causes (and Consequences) of Complacency

If you've read enough business books, you know that a complacent company is a doomed company. BlackBerry grew complacent with its early lead in the smartphone market, and that complacency caused BlackBerry to watch helplessly as Apple and Samsung swept in and took control of the industry BlackBerry created.[6] Blockbuster grew complacent with its business model, and so it reacted too slowly when Netflix and Redbox emerged with a new approach. In a complacent business, innovation slows to a crawl, and eventually that business is left far behind whenever it happens that consumers change

---

[6] As I write, BlackBerry is in the midst of a resurgence, and its stock is among the top performers for the year. If it manages to successfully reinvent itself as a software company or security provider, as it seems to be in the process of doing, that will be an enormous credit to the company; but that success will have no bearing on the fact that its earlier complacency cost it its dominance in the smartphone market.

their tastes, the economy slows, a new technology becomes available, or any other significant event occurs.

Complacency is a risk to us as individuals as well. Studies have shown that people who live in hurricane and tornado zones become less likely to heed disaster warnings the more often they hear those warnings, especially when those warnings result in no or minimal damages. Similarly, HIV-positive patients are increasingly less likely to get tested for the disease today despite the fact that rates of infection are on the rise, a distressing situation attributable in large part to the fact that HIV has become a chronic (as opposed to fatal) condition. When we become complacent, we take fewer precautions and anticipate fewer risks.

However, the *true* danger of complacency is that it is often completely justified. Every winter we're all encouraged to get a flu vaccine, and every winter millions of people choose not to do so and also avoid contracting the flu. Every year someone at your business talks about a potential threat or promising opportunity, and every year several of those threats fail to materialize, and many of those opportunities turn out to be less promising than expected. In these cases, complacency and inaction are a perfectly fine way to behave, which only reinforces our belief that complacency is acceptable. So we're even more complacent the next time around, and the next, and the next, and every time nothing happens our complacency is further justified—until finally something *does* happen, until that threat finally *does* turn into a reality or that disaster finally *does* decide to strike, at which point the most complacent people are left stranded (often literally) while their better-prepared peers and competitors scramble to safety or take advantage of others' helplessness.

Interestingly enough, complacency is caused by exactly one thing and one thing only: repetition. If we hear enough disaster sirens without experiencing an actual disaster, most of us start to slowly ignore the warnings. If a friend of yours complains all the time without ever seeming to do anything about his problems, you will slowly but surely stop lending weight to his complaints. And if your business continues to be profitable year after year after year, you will pay less and less attention to vague mumblings about customer shift or upstart competitors.

Moreover, repetition is a function of time. The more time we have, the more we're able to repeat something. Which means that the Older or more experienced we become, the more likely we are to grow complacent with whatever it is we're currently doing. In general, the more success we've had doing things a certain way, the less value we place on acquiring new skills or changing our approach. Why should we change something that's been so successful for so long?

This tendency toward complacency shouldn't necessarily be interpreted as a critique of Old People, any more than their appreciation of existing practices and processes should necessarily be interpreted as a compliment. These qualities are simply a function of the fact that we get older. As we age, all of us eventually accumulate enough experience and success that we learn to value the systems that have allowed us to achieve that success; and at the same time, all of us tend to downplay new approaches in favor of what we have found to be successful in the past. These predilections are in all of us, and this explains in large part why Young People often come across as impatient (they haven't been around long enough to appreciate the value of existing systems), while Old People often come across as stuck in their ways (they've been around long enough to become complacent with the success they're familiar with).

The Challenge

When it comes to bridging the generational gap regarding the tension between stasis and innovation, you face a two-part challenge. On the one hand, you need to convince Younger or less-experienced people to value and respect existing systems, despite their lack of experience with doing so, and their natural expectation that things will (and should) change more and more quickly all the time. On the other hand, you need to encourage the Old People you work with to resist their natural urge to become complacent with the practices that have contributed to their success up until now. In both cases, you're asking people to actively resist the factors that make most Young People impatient and most Old People complacent.

In other words, you're asking people to engage in deliberate practice, which is the key to becoming an expert performer at anything—ice hockey, ballet, change management, sewing, or adopting innovations. As we pointed out in Chapter 5's discussion of expertise, the *quality* of the practice we engage in is even more important than the quantity of it. To quote Anders Ericsson:

> *We agree that expert performance is qualitatively different from normal performance and even that expert performers have characteristics and abilities that are qualitatively different from or at least outside the range of those of normal adults. However, we deny that these differences are immutable, that is, due to innate talent. Only a few exceptions, most notably height, are genetically prescribed. Instead, we argue that the differences between expert performers and normal adults reflect a life-long period of deliberate effort to improve performance in a specific domain.*

In other words, doing what comes naturally will eventually limit your ability to improve, while forcing yourself to push against your own boundaries will allow you to grow. A chess player who spends 10,000 hours playing against the same opponent will not become a grandmaster. The grandmaster is one who spends 10,000 hours playing different opponents, analyzing different strategies, reading books, studying other people's play, talking with fellow players, and actively resisting the tendency to play an easy game when a harder one will possibly teach him or her something new or better.

That's deliberate practice. And deliberate practice will make your Young People more appreciative of existing systems and your Old People more willing to consider innovative ideas.

So how can you make that happen? How can you encourage your colleagues and employees to deliberately improve when doing so goes against their natural instincts? How can you force people to engage in the kind of intentional, concentrated practice that turns an ordinary athlete into an Olympian? Is it even reasonable to expect your entire team, department, division, or company to be an expert performer, to simultaneously achieve Olympic-grade levels of appreciation for your existing systems *and* the need for constant innovation?

What You Can Do to Inspire Deliberate Practice

In a word, yes, it is reasonable to expect your colleagues to be expert performers. It is possible. It isn't even particularly difficult. And the reason is because stasis, change, and innovation are three of the only things that all of us are experts at. Every one of us has spent our entire lives experiencing success in dozens of different ways. Every one of us has spent our entire lives constantly and continuously changing and innovating—sometimes quickly, sometimes slowly, but always to one degree or another. However, as with many of the things we've discussed in this book, we all tend to forget that about ourselves.

Which means that all you need to do is remind your people of these truths.

Here's how.

As before, the first step to bridging the generational divide with respect to stasis, change, and innovation is to find the areas in which we are all similar so that you can bring everyone you work with closer to Us on the Us/Them line.

Qualities, Attitudes, and Opinions That Young People and Old People Have in Common

1. Change is the natural state, and all of us are constantly incorporating countless changes into our daily lives, both personal and professional. None of us is the same person we were a year ago, and none of us will be the same person a year from now. In exactly the same way, none of us is working in exactly the same way as we were a year ago, and none of us will be working in exactly the same way a year from today.

2. As we experience success or avoid failure, all of us naturally look for ways to replicate that success or continue to prevent that failure. As a result, all of us tend to become complacent with the way we are currently doing things.

As you can see, we are all strikingly similar. If we have been successful—or, at the very least, if we have avoided being unsuccessful—then all of us want to keep doing things the way we've always done them. At the same time, all of us are constantly changing and innovating as a natural consequence of our ever-changing circumstances. This is true across ages, genders, cultures, and historical eras. When it comes to stasis vs. innovation, all of us are overwhelmingly Us.

In fact, the only significant differences between the generations on this point are relatively minor and very easy to manage.

Key Concepts: Why Your Younger or Less-Experienced Colleagues Think and Behave the Way They Do

1. Because Young People have comparatively little experience with the benefits of your existing practices and processes, they are more likely to downplay or dismiss the value of those practices and processes.

2. Today's Young People tend to expect changes to occur quickly and often, in part because they have only ever lived in a world of constant, rapid change. As a result, Young People will tend to agitate for change more often and more quickly than their Older or more-experienced colleagues—not necessarily because they think current practices are failing but because constant change is the only speed they've been trained to understand.

Key Concepts: Why Your Older or More-Experienced Colleagues Think and Behave the Way They Do

1. Because Old People have experienced the benefits of your existing practices and processes, they are *more* likely to value those practices and processes and *less* likely to see the need to replace them with an untested approach.

2. Because complacency is a function of time, experience, and repetition, Old People are at greater risk of falling into complacent behaviors than their Younger counterparts.

In many ways, this isn't a generational issue at all. There's nothing inherent in Traditionalists, Baby Boomers, Gen Xers, or Millennials that makes an entire group of people cautious, rigid, adventurous, flexible, or anything else. Our attitude toward stasis, change, and innovation is the predictable result of the way we all evolve as we age and acquire experience. There's nothing new happening today that hasn't been happening for centuries. The rise of technology and the Internet may have accentuated the natural division between more- and less-experienced people, but this tension has existed for as long as human beings have been around.

It might sound daunting that we've been dealing with these issues throughout human history, but that actually makes the solutions a lot easier because all you need to do is what people have been doing all along: encourage your Young People to see things from the perspective of their Older or more-experienced colleagues and vice versa. All it takes is to get people to put themselves in someone else's shoes, pure and simple. Nothing you need to do here will require a new strategy of any kind.

Perhaps you want to convince your employees or colleagues to continue doing something you've been doing in exactly the same way for the past decade. Or perhaps you want to encourage someone who's been doing the same thing for a decade to consider a new approach. Either way, here's what you can do. And again (I'm sure you're tired of hearing this by now, but I can't stop myself), none of this is going to cost you anything.

Strategies to Illustrate the Importance of Stasis and Innovation

- **Explain to your Young colleagues and employees** why **you do things the way you do.** If you've been around for a while, then it's probably obvious to you why your business operates the way it does. But to Young People in general and new employees in particular, nothing is obvious. That's not their fault; they simply don't have the same experience you do. So when they ask why you do things a certain way, don't immediately interpret their questions as a personal attack; instead look at those questions as an honest attempt to learn more about how your business works. The more you're able to explain the rationale behind what you do, the more buy-in you'll get from everyone. And if you *can't* offer a good explanation for why you do things the way that you do, then it's quite possible your current approach isn't as perfect as it could be.

- **Find examples to illustrate how all of us sometimes benefit from doing things the way we've always done them.** Sometimes one of your colleagues or employees (more often than not a Young Person) will stubbornly refuse to see the value of your approach to business, even after you've explained the rationale behind it. If that happens, then you're facing a person who tends to believe that new systems are always better than existing ones. So prove the person wrong. Point out the benefits of calling a customer over emailing or texting, or ask the person to outline all the advantages of an on-site safety inspection that can't be replicated with a computer program. And if all that fails, challenge the person to try things your way for a specified period of time and then write a report afterward about all the benefits and drawbacks of doing things your way. You'll basically be daring your colleague to come up with a better way of doing business while forcing him or her to acknowledge the need to be intimately familiar with the way things are currently done. At the end of this process, your initially resistant Young Person will almost certainly wind up realizing at least some of the benefits of your current practices and processes—and you might end up realizing various improvements you might be able to make. It's a guaranteed win–win.

- **Remind change-averse people that they have been changing constantly throughout their entire personal and professional lives.** When changes become necessary— or, worse, when changes are forced upon us—some people are bound to dig in their heels and fight against implementation with everything they have. (More often than not, this will be an Older or more-experienced person.) However, each one of those people has been changing his or her entire life, and it should be easy for you to point out a few of those changes. Promotions, new responsibilities, new technologies, new government regulations, new customers, new budgets—even the most change-averse person in your company has dealt with and survived every one of those changes, and many of them have probably happened in the past couple years. If you're able to frame the current change as a continuation of the natural evolution of business rather than as a jarring detour on an otherwise unbroken road, you'll erode the resistance of even the most obstinate of your colleagues and employees, and they'll at least be forced to listen to you with an open mind. We come back to this concept in the next chapter as well.

- **Use a previous failure to illustrate the occasional value of "business as usual."** Once again, we're anticipating the next chapter, but there's no better use for failures than as educational opportunities. If one of your Young colleagues or employees insists that change at all costs is the only way to go, point out any instance where that proved not to be true. Unless you've succeeded at blocking those memories entirely, it shouldn't be hard to find a few things that didn't go the way you wanted them to, and each one of them can help reinforce how smart it might be to stick with your existing strategies. As with the idea just previously discussed, you may not get complete and unqualified agreement, but your people will at least be forced to listen to you with an open mind.

- **Impress upon everyone the reality that change is occurring faster now than it used to.** Our technological revolution has guaranteed the truth of this, and there is zero chance we're going to return to a slower way of doing things. However, many people have been given the "things are happening faster now than ever" platitude without being given any concrete proof of that statement. So use the examples in this book or come up with some examples specific to your business that will illustrate the truth of our accelerated world. Some of your people might not like this new hyperactive reality; but if you can get them to concede that it *is* the reality, they are far more likely to keep an open mind the next time you discuss a new policy or computer system six months after implementing the last one.

- **Work every day toward creating a culture that actively opposes the urge toward complacency.** This is a difficult one because it may involve changing or modifying your existing work culture, and that always takes time. Young People are often complacent in their belief that change is invariably a positive, while Old People are often complacent in their belief that existing approaches are invariably the best ones. Both attitudes are misguided, and so it's important to remind people on a regular basis how dangerous that can be. So celebrate successes and then gently mention that no success is guaranteed to last forever, or encourage your employees to engage in continuing education. If you put safety signs or motivational posters around your office, make sure you change them from time to time so that people don't get in the habit of ignoring those messages. Most importantly, do what you can to convince your team that nobody is always right 100% of the time. There are easy ways to prove that, and we talk about that in more detail in the next chapter.

When it comes to stasis vs. innovation, the most important point is that last one: Nobody is always right 100% of the time. Sometimes business as usual is the best course of action, and sometimes change is necessary. It shouldn't be too difficult to provide examples of the value of both approaches, and by doing so, you'll be bringing everyone closer together on the Us/Them spectrum.

However, doing so will only solve the change management problem in theory, and theory is a bit different than practice. In theory, I am the best tennis player in the world, given that I have never lost a match, and every professional tennis player has lost several of them. However, I've also never gotten around to testing that theory since I've never bothered to play tennis, and I've got a sneaking suspicion that my theory might not hold up if I were to give it a shot.

Similarly, getting Young People and Old People to agree that none of them is always right is one thing. But it's another thing entirely to get them all to agree when you're talking about a specific procedure, purchase, policy, or anything else. Fortunately for you, my publishers threatened me with death if I didn't write a chapter about it, so I went ahead and did it.

Key Strategies for Resolving Issues with Your Younger or Less-Experienced Colleagues

(Reproduced from Chapters 4 and 5)

1. Present your new hires with business cards on their first day of work.

2. Invite your newest employees or team members to deliver a presentation to the rest of your team on a topic they already know something about.

3. Learn their names quickly, call them by name when you say hello, and praise them as often as you can think to.

4. If you are in a supervisory role, tell everyone who directly reports to you that you will go to bat for them if necessary.

5. Solicit the opinions of everyone who directly reports to you on a regular basis.

6. Invite your colleagues and employees to lunch on a weekly or monthly basis.

7. If you are a supervisor or manager, ask them what they want out of their jobs *over and above* the salary and benefits your company provides.

8. Offer your services as a mentor or create a mentorship program.

9. Give them the opportunity to use their skills and abilities on a regular basis.

10. If you have some young colleagues or employees with substandard work ethics, compare their careers to other common experiences they may be familiar with.

11. Share your own path to professional success with your young colleagues or employees.

12. Instill an appreciation for delayed gratification by presenting the impending retirement of your older workers as an opportunity for your younger workers.

13. Periodically highlight examples of people who succeeded after repeated failures or other setbacks.

14. Emphasize the similarities between professional and personal successes.

15. Point out, when applicable, that age and experience are not *always* correlated.

16. If necessary, fire your young employees quickly.

(Chapter 6)

17. Explain to Young People why **you do things the way you do.**

18. Find examples to illustrate how all of us sometimes benefit from doing things the way we've always done them.

19. Use a previous failure to illustrate the occasional value of "business as usual."

20. Impress upon everyone the reality that change is occurring faster now than it used to.

21. Work every day to create a culture that actively opposes the urge toward complacency.

Key Strategies for Resolving Issues with Your Older or More-Experienced Colleagues

(Reproduced from Chapters 4 and 5)

1. If you are in a supervisory role, tell everyone who directly reports to you that you will go to bat for them if necessary.

2. Solicit the opinions of everyone who directly reports to you on a regular basis.

3. Invite your colleagues and employees to lunch on a weekly or monthly basis.

4. Ask your colleagues and employees why they have stayed with your company as long as they have.

5. If you are a supervisor or manager, ask your colleagues and employees what they want out of their jobs *over and above* the salary and benefits your company provides.

6. Give your colleagues and employees the opportunity to use their skills and abilities on a regular basis.

7. Tell your manager or other senior employees that you intend to spend your career working your way up the ladder at your company.

8. Find an older or more-experienced person and ask him or her to be your mentor.

9. If you are younger or more inexperienced than most of your colleagues, make it clear that you are prepared to work hard.

10. Periodically highlight examples of people who succeeded after repeated failures or other setbacks.

11. Emphasize the similarities between professional and personal success.

12. Point out, when applicable, that age and experience are not *always* correlated.

13. If necessary, encourage your older employees into early retirement.

(Chapter 6)

14. **Remind change-averse people that they have been changing constantly throughout their entire personal and professional lives.**

15. **Impress upon everyone the reality that change is occurring faster now than it used to.**

16. **Work every day to create a culture that actively opposes the urge toward complacency.**

7

Deciding How (or Whether) to Implement a Change

You now know why some of your colleagues are constantly agitating for change while others are constantly resisting it. You understand why this difference tends to break along generational lines, and you know how to explain the value of your existing systems and also how to remind people that change and innovation have always been a natural part of their careers. In theory, there really shouldn't be any more problems.

Liesl A. is 59 years old and manages a factory in Germany for a multinational auto manufacturer. In her own words:

> Six weeks ago we got a new VP of operations, and his first order of business was to implement an overhaul to our design process. Each of our plants is responsible for creating separate elements of the vehicles we build, and while most of them use the same computer programs to create the designs, which makes it fairly easy to share specs from one facility to another, a few of them are still operating on older systems. That inconsistency had occasionally led to problems and delays in the past, and our new VP wanted to correct that.
>
> Most of us were expecting that the factories using the older software would be forced to upgrade to the systems that the majority of the plants were already using. My colleagues at those facilities were already voicing their opposition, since they were familiar with their systems, and an upgrade would

require a lot of training on their end. But it made sense for all of us to use the same software, so I was fairly certain it would go through.

However, our new VP had a completely different idea. He wanted us to all use the same software, but he wanted to upgrade every facility to a completely new system. When he called an all-hands meeting to show us what that system was, I was quite frankly shocked. It was like nothing we had ever seen, a fully holographic display that you could actually stand inside of in order to see the design. A few of my colleagues had read about it, but none of us had seen it in person. It was beautiful, and there was no denying that it had some major advantages over what we were all accustomed to. But it would also require a physical installation in each of our facilities, which would be enormously expensive—and it was a relatively new software, which meant all kinds of opportunities for bugs and problems that would potentially cause even more delays than what we were currently dealing with.

To say that this idea has been controversial is putting it lightly. It's pretty much the only thing any of us has talked about for the past month. Half of us think it's the way of the future, and half of us think it will be the worst software implementation in the history of our company.

But theory often breaks down when we're talking about specific real-world situations. Even if you're successful at convincing everyone that change is a natural process we're all experiencing every day of our lives, you'll still run into resistance when you try to implement a new policy, procedure, or product. So why doesn't philosophy align with action? Why would someone—Young Person or Old Person—acknowledge the need for change in theory but still fight it in practice?

As with everything else we've discussed in this book, there's a very logical reason for it. And given that I wore a full-body chicken suit on a semi-regular basis in my youth,[1] I think it best to start explaining that reason by looking at the world through the lens of fashion.

---

[1] True story. You'll have to ask me about it sometime.

What Does Fashion Have to Do with Changes in My Business?

Let's hop back to the 1950s for a moment. Perhaps you can remember the prevailing fashions of the day, or perhaps you've only seen it in movies. The 1950s were a conservative time. Men wore hats and suits and polished their shoes; women sported dresses and attended carefully to their hair. Everywhere you looked, people took pride in maintaining an elegant appearance, even in casual settings. Indeed, even gas station attendants ironed their uniforms and kept them pressed and starched. Obviously, this isn't how everyone dressed in the 1950s, but this is the fashion ideal that has been passed down from that decade.

Flash forward to the 1960s, however, and you get a different ideal. Flip-flops and tie-dye shirts, dreadlocks and shorts, sleeveless tank tops and the kind of beards that Middle Earth's dwarves would envy. Women sometimes wrapped curtains around themselves and called them dresses, and men sometimes decided that pants were optional. Today's Old People often decry the sloppy fashions of Young People while forgetting that theirs was the first generation in modern times to make such sloppiness fashionable. Again, this isn't how everyone dressed in the 1960s...but whatever idea we have of 1950s fashion, 1960s fashion is the opposite of that.

And then things just got weird. The 1970s was all horsehair boots and plaid leisure suits, since women apparently all wanted to look like go-go dancers and men wanted to look like they were wearing their grandparents' tablecloths. The 1980s brought denim jackets and leg warmers and slitted sunglasses and shiny leather pants, and women everywhere shot a gallon of hairspray into their hair every morning to create bangs a tornado couldn't touch. The 1990s brought us the unemployed lumberjack, ripped jeans and flannel shirts as far as the eye could see.

And as for today, I will just say that in the past month I have seen people working away at their jobs while wearing the following: a woman with pink hair and one blue eyebrow; a woman with 14 or 15 facial piercings and half of her head shaved; a man in a fedora, three-piece burgundy suit, and bowling shoes; a woman in a t-shirt, slippers, and pajama pants; a man in linen yoga pants held in place by a piece of rope; an impeccably dressed woman with one arm fully tattooed; and a man named Kyle wearing a button-down shirt he bought at a consignment store specifically because it had the name "Billy" monogrammed on the left breast pocket and he thought it was funny. As best as I can tell, today's fashion ethos is suffering from multiple personality disorder.

There are two important things to take away from the evolution of fashion over the past 60 years. The first is that the dress code issue, which you've probably been grappling with and which in many ways is the quintessential generational difference in the workplace, is not a new phenomenon. Today's Millennials are not pushing the boundaries of acceptable dress any differently than Baby Boomers did in the 1960s and 1970s, or Gen Xers in the 1980s and 1990s. Instead, Young People have been continuously challenging established fashions since at least the late 1950s. This is a small point, but it's important for reinforcing the main theme of this book: The generational issues you're facing at work are not significantly different from the generational issues people have always faced, and those issues break more commonly in two categories than four.

But there is a broader point to this walk down memory lane. Based on what I've just written, it might seem as though fashion is changing all the time, a constant progression from old to new. However, that's not really true. Because if you consider what comprises the standard business outfit today, it's not fundamentally different from the standard business outfit of the 1950s. There are differences, of course; people more commonly wear tennis shoes today, men can choose not to wear a tie and still look perfectly professional, and women are just as likely to wear pants as skirts. But a side-by-side comparison of a proper 1950s businessperson and a proper 2015 businessperson will reveal far more similarities than differences.

Therefore, over the past 60 years, most of our fashion experiments have turned out to be nothing more than passing fads. There is no real place for tie-dye shirts in the business world, or leisure suits, or ripped jeans, or many of the other styles that have been very popular at various times. In fact, the majority of these fashion "innovations" have made exactly zero impact on our conception of acceptable business attire. For 60 years we have taken fashion detours that have ultimately led to dead ends, and we have stayed more or less true to the 1950s idea of what constitutes professional dress.

Why Some People Resist New Ideas

Why have I spent so long describing the evolution of fashion over the past 60 years? Because the evolution of fashion is a perfect example to explain why people sometimes resist new ideas—namely, because many new ideas end up being unsuccessful. Sometimes new products are wildly popular for a month or a year and then disappear. Sometimes new initiatives are great on paper but fail miserably when put into practice. Sometimes plans turn out to be five times as expensive as expected. In other words, sometimes new ideas simply don't work as well as they're supposed to, and you would be far better off ignoring them and sticking with whatever it is you're currently doing.

But you don't have to take my word for it. Consider the following examples:

- In 1980, Pioneer introduced the laserdisc for use in the home market as a direct challenge to VCRs, which first came to market in 1977.[2] It featured a superior picture quality to VHS tapes (400 horizontal lines vs. 250), the ability to jump instantaneously to any point in a movie without the need to rewind, and more audio channels. Laserdiscs were also heavier and bulkier than VHS tapes, stored less data, and didn't allow for recording or overwriting. Consumers overwhelmingly choose convenience and recordability over higher quality; annual laserdisc player sales peaked at 2 million units in the United States, compared to 11 million VCR sales in 1985, 9.8 million in 1988, and 9.5 million in 1989.

- The 1990s saw skyrocketing popularity of both mobile phones and mobile video game systems. These devices were separate, however, so consumers had to carry both of them. In

---

[2] The original VCR cost between $1,000 and $1,400, by the way—more than twice as much as the original iPad.

2003, Nokia introduced the N-Gage as a dual-platform device, capable of making phone calls and playing high-quality video games. Gamers could even play one another through Bluetooth connections. The idea was an excellent one, as shown by the fact that gaming is a key feature of every modern smartphone. However, it was an idea ahead of its time. Because touchscreen technology had not yet been developed, the N-Gage required consumers to use the phone keypad as the video game controls; the alternative would have been to put both phone buttons and video game controls side-by-side on the same device, which would have been prohibitively bulky. Unfortunately for Nokia, users found the gaming setup to be difficult and unintuitive and the device itself to be awkward for receiving phone calls. In the year of its release, the Nokia N-Gage was outsold 100-to-1 by the Nintendo GameBoy Advance.

- In February 1999, Flooz.com launched. A precursor to Bitcoin, Flooz attempted to create a completely new, online-only currency that could be purchased and then redeemed with participating Internet retailers. The only problem was that there was absolutely no reason to choose Flooz over credit cards, gift cards, and other established forms of payment—unless you wanted to launder money by transferring it to a fictitious currency and then changing it back, which by mid-2001 is how 19% of Flooz.com transactions were categorized. The company announced its closure on August 26, 2001, having spent between $35 and $50 million in venture capital.

- In January 1998, eight months before Google existed, Disney decided to make a foray into online search and launched Go.com. Intended to compete with Yahoo! and Alta Vista, Go.com was supposed to be a comprehensive search engine that would benefit from the advertising dollars that made (and still make) search engines so profitable. However, being a Disney property meant that Go.com had to filter out any content deemed too mature, inappropriate, or otherwise inconsistent with the Disney brand. As a result, Go.com was doomed from the start to be a semi-functional search engine at best. That, combined with the fact that Internet users wanted to access online content directly instead of having to stare at Disney ads before they could reach whatever they were searching for (ever wonder why Google's homepage is so sparse?), led to the closure of Go.com in January 2001—at a loss of $790 million.

- In 2003, Myspace was founded and quickly became the most popular social media platform in existence—so successful, in fact, that barely two years later, Rupert Murdoch's News Corporation bought Myspace for $580 million in a heated bidding war with Viacom.[3] At the time, everyone thought it a great purchase—and, indeed, the next couple years justified News Corp.'s optimism: In 2006 Myspace surpassed Google as the most-visited website on the planet, and in 2007 Myspace was valued at $12 billion. And then, for numerous reasons that would require another book to fully explain, people started abandoning Myspace as quickly as they had joined. By 2011, the company's fortunes had fallen so far that News Corp. decided to sell Myspace to Specific Media, an investment group led by Justin Timberlake, for $35 million—6% of what they had paid for it a mere five years earlier. Rupert Murdoch later called the acquisition of Myspace a "huge mistake."

- In 1993, Ty Warner, Inc., released the first nine Beanie Babies in what would eventually become an armada. The toys became wildly popular, and Ty's policy of limiting production and systematically retiring various models convinced many people that Beanie Babies would rise in value. People begin to collect the $5 toys as part of their investment portfolio, and for a time, many sought-after Beanie Babies sold for hundreds or even thousands of dollars. As late as 1998, one influential magazine devoted to the Beanie Baby market projected that an "investment grade" Stripes the Dark Tiger was worth $250 and would be worth $1,000 in 2008. Then it all collapsed, as quickly and completely as the housing bubble in 2007. Today Stripes is selling for less than 1% of his projected 2008 value, and at least one documentary ("Bankrupt by Beanies") testifies to the hundreds of thousands of dollars some investors lost as a result.

---

[3] Viacom's failure to acquire Myspace led to the firing of its then-CEO, Tom Freston.

This list could continue infinitely, but the point is clear: New ideas sometimes fail. It's as simple as that. We all know it, we've all seen it, and we've all dealt with the aftermath of a healthy number of bad decisions. So sometimes we resist the next new idea because we don't wish to repeat the experience of living through yet another failure.

In fact, aversion to change is more a consequence of our outlook than it is our age or experience level. All of us start accumulating failures as soon as we're born—burning ourselves on hot stoves, falling off of bicycles, failing exams, quitting piano lessons, and so on. By the time we enter our working lives, all of us have experienced plenty of failure at plenty of different things, and that causes many of us to approach the next new thing with some degree of trepidation. You've almost certainly worked with both Young People and Old People who were resistant to new ideas. You can probably think of some Old People who automatically say no to any new suggestion that comes their way, and you've probably worked with some Young People who were even more stuck in their ways than most of their Older or more-experienced peers. And in every case, regardless of the age of the person in question, their attitude is a direct consequence of focusing on the potential risks rather than the potential rewards. All of us do this from time to time.

However, the stereotype still exists that Old People are more reluctant to change than Young People. Why would this be true? If aversion to change is more a function of attitude than anything else, why would Old People be more resistant to it than Young People?

Easy—because they're *older*. In the Chapter 6, we discussed how repeated success (or repeated non-failure) causes all of us to trend toward complacency as we age. At the same time, all of us *also* accumulate a larger body of failures as we age. The older we get, the more fads we've seen come and go, and the more ideas we've been exposed to that didn't work out the way they were supposed to. And just as exposure to repeated success leads to complacency, exposure to repeated failure leads to caution and skepticism. It would have to, unless you're somehow immune or indifferent to the negative effects of all those failures—and very few of us are. Thus, because a 60-year-old will inevitably have experienced more successes and failures than a 25-year-old, the 60-year-old is more likely to be complacent in his or her successes and more cautious as a result of his or her greater number of failures. This isn't a hard-and-fast rule, of course, since people have an annoying habit of not fitting perfectly into definitional boxes, but it *is* a tendency that comes as we accumulate both age and experience.

In fact, one of the biggest advantages that Old People bring to the professional world is the perspective they have acquired by virtue of getting older and accumulating more experience. In many cases, they aren't theorizing about the potential problems that will come from a new idea or initiative; often they're making direct comparisons between today's idea and one they experienced personally a few years ago. Indeed, without the perspective that Old People bring to the table, every new idea would be based entirely on educated guesses rather than on anything concrete.

So if you share a new idea with Older or more-experienced colleagues and run into some resistance, you're welcome to assume that they're intentionally trying to be spiteful. They very well could hate you and everything you've ever thought. It's far more likely, though, that they're simply trying to avoid making a bad decision. Perhaps your idea reminds them of something they tried years ago that didn't work out very well. Maybe they aren't convinced that the theoretical and untested advantages of your approach are better than the known and well-tested advantages of their current approach. Whatever the reasons behind their hesitation, their ultimate goal is almost always to avoid making a mistake—and it's critical that you encourage those people to voice their concerns because their uncertainty will require you to analyze your new ideas in ways that you may not have done otherwise.

In Her Own Words: Danielle G. on Watching a New Idea Fail

Danielle G. is 40 years old and has worked for the past 11 years at a large consulting company. In her own words:

> Most of our business involves consultant teams flying to our clients' operational centers for in-person training and strategy meetings. It's expensive for our customers, and despite

the fact that we pay our consultants well, we still experience higher turnover than we'd like because the constant travel eventually wears on most of them. So when one of my direct reports suggested that we package some of our materials into an online training platform for our clients, I thought it was a great idea. We could reduce the barrier to entry for our services by starting clients on an inexpensive online platform and then moving them over time to our bread-and-butter business, and we could hopefully lower our attrition by reducing travel time.

However, when we presented this idea to my boss, he said very simply, "It won't work." I argued my case over the next couple weeks, and eventually he relented enough to let us put together a demo program that we could show to some of our existing clients to gauge their interest. If the feedback we got was positive, we'd move it up the ladder and talk about a full-scale implementation.

I won't bore you with the details, so let me just say that we spent three months of after-hours time putting together the demo program. I was excited as I became more and more certain that our imminent success would be a huge boost to our careers.

So imagine our disappointment when exactly zero of our clients showed any interest. They found our online training too generic for their purposes, which in hindsight makes sense since we were trying to create one program to service dozens of unrelated industries. Also, it turns out that they preferred in-person consultation, and they felt the premium they paid for it was worth the return. I was forced to report back to my boss that the experiment had been a complete failure.

Fortunately for me, my boss didn't see it that way. He told me that our company had tried something very similar in the 1990s, only much larger and far more expensive. The results had been a total failure. He said, "It's good to know that our core business still resonates with our clients, and you were able to verify that for us at a minimum of time and money. I consider that a win." I'm very grateful he had that attitude. He turned what could have been humiliating into a very positive learning experience.

And Now, the Other Side of the Coin

So there you have it: Many new ideas don't work out. That's why people are often averse to change, and that's why you should never try anything new ever again.

There are only two tiny problems with that approach. First, it's completely impossible. And second, some new ideas actually end up being *good* ones. In fact, for every example of people embracing a new idea only to be disappointed when the idea fails to live up to its potential, there is a different example of people resisting a new idea only to be shocked and amazed when that new idea proves to be revolutionary.

But again, don't take my word for it. Consider these examples:

- In the late 1990s, an electronics engineer named Tony Fadell had an idea. Since 1995 he had been working on handheld devices at Philips, and he thought people would like a digital music player that could fit into your hand. He presented the idea to executives at Philips, who showed no interest. So in July 1999 he founded his own company, Fuse, to develop the product. He failed to secure enough funding, however, so Fuse went under, and Fadell decided to try partnering with another company to build his product. In 2000 he approached Real Networks with his idea for a handheld digital music player, but executives there also showed no interest. Then, in 2001, Fadell spoke with Steve Jobs and learned that Apple was in the initial stages of developing a product very similar to the one Fadell had in mind. Fadell was hired and ultimately picked to lead the team that would develop the first iPod. Executives at both Philips and Real Networks had passed on an idea that would earn billions.

- In the 2000 NFL draft, Tom Brady was chosen in the seventh round, which is a polite way of saying that every NFL team rejected him six times before the New England Patriots decided he was better than whoever else was left over. In the 14 years since, he has led the Patriots to six Super Bowls, four of which the team has won. By comparison, of the six quarter-backs picked before Tom Brady in the 2000 draft (Chad Pennington, Giovanni Carmazzi, Chris Redman, Tee Martin, Marc Bulger, and Spurgeon Wynn), only Chris Redman has a Super Bowl ring, which he earned as a backup in his rookie season.

- In 1918, French general Ferdinand Foch was appointed commander-in-chief of the Allied Armies. He had impeccable military credentials, and many historians credit him with having devised the strategies that would ultimately win the war against Germany. However, in 1904, when presented with reports of the first airplanes, he stated unequivocally, "Airplanes are interesting toys but of no military value." Without air support, Foch's offensive of September 26, 1918, would very likely not have been as successful as it was.

- In 1880 Henry Morton, the president of the Stevens Institute of Technology, offered this prediction upon hearing of Thomas Edison's electric lightbulb: "Everyone acquainted with the subject will recognize it as a conspicuous failure."

- Lord Kelvin, one of the most highly respected scientists of his time, said in 1897, "Radio has no future."

- In February 2005, as the popularity of his social media platform was skyrocketing, Myspace cofounder and CEO Chris DeWolfe met with Mark Zuckerberg to discuss Myspace's acquisition of Facebook. At the time, Facebook was primarily used by college students and was significantly smaller than Myspace. Zuckerberg offered to sell Facebook for $75 million, and DeWolfe refused. He saw no need to pay such an absurd amount of money for a social media platform that would only ever be used by college students. Besides, he thought, Facebook was more of a novelty than a real threat.

- In 1970 Bernard Sadow, a vice president for a luggage company, was returning from a vacation when he became frustrated by his heavy and cumbersome luggage. Observing an airport worker with a wheeled skid, he hit upon the idea of attaching wheels to luggage, which he did originally by removing the casters from a wardrobe and attaching a strap to the front of his suitcase.[4] His was at least the third attempt at putting wheels on luggage; a wheeled trunk had been patented in 1887 and a wheeled suitcase in 1945, but neither invention took off. At first, Sadow's invention suffered the same fate; retailer after retailer refused to carry it, primarily arguing (this is completely true) that wheeling luggage around wasn't something that a grown man would ever do. "People do not accept change well," Sadow said of the experience. It took almost two years for Sadow's wheeled luggage to find its first advocate in Macy's.

But Sadow's invention still didn't revolutionize the luggage industry. People bought wheeled luggage when Macy's first made it available in 1972, but it didn't become a ubiquitous sight at airports around the world. That would have to wait until 1987, when an airline pilot named Robert Plath took his own luggage into his garage workshop and created the Rollaboard, a rolling suitcase with a retractable handle. Other luggage companies took no notice. Plath initially sold his invention to fellow pilots and other airline workers, but travelers began asking where they could get the same for themselves. Plath then quit flying and started his own luggage company, Travelpro International. Only after Rollaboards had become popular did other luggage companies take notice and begin to create their own versions.

Like the previous list, this one could continue indefinitely.[5] Every type of business—indeed, every company—has its share of people far too comfortable with their current success who refused to see the potential of industry-changing innovations when they were first presented. This is probably most common with technological

---

[4] Prior to this, one of the most popular solutions of the 1960s was to purchase a wheeled folding cart. Travelers could unfold the cart, place their luggage on it, wheel it wherever they wanted, and then fold the cart up and strap it to the luggage once they got to their destination. The wheels were *RIGHT THERE!!!!!* And yet nobody thought to put the two of them together.

[5] I'm certain that a loooong time ago, whenever the first human being put on clothing, other naked people were sitting around saying, "That's never going to work. He looks ridiculous. Seriously (gesturing to naked self), who would want to cover all this up?"

advancements, as I have personally spoken to people who swore they would quit their jobs rather than use a computer, stop using DOS, take work home on a laptop, put up with email on their phones, or engage in any form of social media. You probably know some of those people. You've probably *been* one of those people at one time or another. Yet all those changes came, and it is now impossible for us to imagine doing business the way we used to.

So if one of your colleagues is insistent on getting you to agree how wonderful his or her new idea is, you're welcome to assume that he's tacitly calling everything you've ever done a complete failure. He very well could hate you and everything you've ever thought.[6] It's far more likely, though, that he's simply excited about capitalizing on a possible opportunity. He may have been studying the market when you weren't looking. If it's a new colleague making the suggestion, he may have seen something you haven't needed to see because your track record of success may have made it less important for you to look for something new. Whatever the reasons for his enthusiasm, his ultimate goal is very likely to help your company become even more successful than it already is—and it's critical that you encourage such people to share their ideas because those new concepts will require you to analyze your business in ways that you may not have done otherwise.

In His Own Words: Desmond Y. on Forcing Himself to Change

Desmond Y. is 59 years old and has worked his entire career at a Fortune 1000 company. In his own words:

> When I hired in, my company was just making the transition to DOS. Most of my bosses were used to punch cards and were angry about having to adjust. I'd learned DOS in college and so was excited about working for a progressive company. I decided my bosses were just stubborn and lazy.

---

[6] It sounds more absurd the more times you read it, doesn't it?

Thirty-six years later, my company announced that it was going to roll out a new ERP system, and I thought it was ridiculous and unnecessary. I said as much to one of my peers, expecting him to agree with me, but instead he said, "Well, it beats punch cards." He didn't mean anything by the comment—it was just a throwaway joke, really—but somehow it made me realize that I was doing the same thing my bosses had done 36 years before, when we were rolling out DOS. I promised to stop complaining right then and to embrace the change even if it killed me.

It took about five months for me to learn everything I needed to, and it wasn't fun. But I can say with all honesty now that our new system is significantly better than what we had been using. I wish I could apologize to my old bosses for some of the things I thought about them.

Every business, at every point in its existence, is engaged in a constant battle between sticking with existing practices and trying to anticipate the needs of the unknown market the future is going to bring. Some new ideas are terrible, while others are revolutionary. Some new initiatives will fail, and others will become industry standard. Unfortunately, it's impossible to predict with perfect accuracy which changes will take off and which ones won't; and for that reason, it is also impossible to get 100% agreement on adopting a new and untested idea. Some people are going to focus more on the potential risks, while others will focus more on the potential rewards, and there's no getting around that.

So What Can You Do?

That last bit may have upset you. This book has promised to help you resolve every generational issue you'll ever face, and now you're being told that you'll never get 100% buy-in on whether to adopt a new initiative or keep doing things the way you've been doing them. Did I lie to you, then? Did I just throw that onto the cover to trick you into reading this stupid thing?

No, because this *isn't* a generational issue at all. When it comes to addressing the potential merits and drawbacks of a specific new idea, product, or process, the only generational factor at play is our tendency as we age to become more cautious with respect to new ideas and more comfortable with respect to established practices—and we've already discussed how to address that issue. Otherwise, any frustration you've experienced regarding the adoption or rejection of specific initiatives comes from exactly two sources:

- Some people focus on the potential positive outcomes expected to come from the adoption of the new idea, while others focus on the potential negative outcomes.
- Some people focus on the positive consequences of staying with an existing system, while others focus on the negative consequences.

This tension has nothing to do with generational characteristics and everything to do with our different personalities. There are people of all ages who are naturally adventurous and conservative. You'll almost certainly have both Young People and Old People who are convinced that a new idea is going to be fantastic, and you'll just as certainly have both Young People and Old People who are perfectly happy to do whatever work is necessary to adopt a new idea but who still think you should stick with whatever you're doing now.

Let's take the dress code issue mentioned in Matthew's story back in Chapter 1. If you've experienced the same issue, then you already know that this is almost exclusively the consequence of Young People choosing to dress in ways that some Old People disapprove of. I have delivered hundreds of keynote presentations to virtually every kind of company and industry imaginable, and I've found that when it comes to generational tension, the issue of dress seems to cause more frustration than any other single issue.

The primary reason this seemingly small difference is such a contentious one is that Young People typically want to dress casually because they feel like it, and Old People typically want everyone to dress more formally because they prefer it—at least, that's how the conversation usually goes, if indeed there's any conversation at all. In both cases, the attitude is virtually identical: *Everyone should do things my way because that's how I like it.* This approach is guaranteed to resolve exactly nothing.

Now I've already made the argument that this issue has been continuous and unbroken since at least World War II. When they were younger, today's Baby Boomers dressed in ways their elders found scandalously unprofessional. ("You're not going to wear a suit to work? You're not going to wear a tie? How will anyone take you seriously?") When Gen Xers were younger, they dressed in ways many Baby Boomers found absurd. ("You want to wear sneakers with dress pants? You think that gives a good impression?") With respect to dress, Millennials are behaving no differently than Young People have for generations. But does that knowledge do anything to solve the actual disagreement between people who believe in adhering to different dress codes? Absolutely not.

Instead, if any reconciliation and consensus are ever going to occur, then all concerned parties will need to be able to say what benefits they believe will result from their ideas or approach. Is there any indication that professional dress leads to higher productivity or a stronger work culture? Is there any evidence that relaxing your dress code will improve employee morale? Do you work in direct contact with your customers and so have reason to believe that physical appearance is an important element in successfully conducting business? If you can't come up with reasons for wanting to do things your way, then you're either sticking with an existing practice out of habit or advocating for a new practice because you find it interesting somehow, and neither approach will convince anyone else that your way is a good one.

It is both impossible and unreasonable to expect that everyone you work with will enthusiastically support every new thing that comes along, and no amount of conversation is going to change that. All of us have opinions, and many of us are rather attached to our own ideas of how things should be done. But if everyone has the opportunity to explain the benefits they think will come from either adopting a new approach or keeping things the way they are, then two things will happen. First, you (and everyone else) will know the reasons some people disagree with you, which will automatically make the disagreement less intense and more civil. And second, everyone will know what the goals are for either implementing or not implementing the change in question. If a change occurs and people start to see the benefits that its advocates predicted, then those who resisted will slowly admit the value of the change; and if you continue with "business as usual" and keep finding success in the ways its advocates promised, then those who wanted to change will slowly concede the value of your existing approach. Either way, you will have invited everyone to participate, and there's no better way to bring people closer together on the Us/Them spectrum than by making them realize that they all have something to contribute.

Strategies for Successfully Adopting (or Rejecting) a New Idea

- **Be able to explain *specifically* how you believe a new initiative will improve business.** "It's just better" is not an argument, and it's not likely to win over any detractors. New ideas need to be accompanied with concrete arguments to support their utility. For example:

  - "If we make these changes to the script our call center workers are using, we'll be able to reduce their average call time by 43 seconds, which will save us $85,000 in reduced operating costs—plus it will make our customers 43 seconds happier."

  - "Our hotel nightclub makes 75% of its revenue on Thursday through Saturday nights, but 55% of our clientele are here between Sunday and Thursday. If we come up with some new activities for those four off-days, we'll be able to capitalize on a huge market—and we won't have to advertise any differently because those people are already staying on our property."

  - "I've talked informally with several people on this floor, and many of them feel that they'd be able to do their jobs more effectively if they could have two computer monitors. I know it would be an extra expense, but it might be worth it for the extra productivity we'd get."

  As you can see, this approach often implies that you've done some research to validate the utility of your new idea. And this is exactly as it should be. The more research you're able to do, the more confident you can be that the decision you're making is the right one. Either that or you'll find that your initial enthusiasm was misplaced in a "solution" whose value falls apart upon closer study, which is an outcome that's almost as good. After all, when would you rather learn that a new idea isn't going to work—during the planning phases or six months after it's been implemented?

- **Be able to explain *specifically* how you believe sticking with an existing strategy is the best approach.** I don't want to beat a dead horse,[7] so I'm not going to repeat everything I just wrote. However, some examples might be useful:

  - "I realize that we can't afford to get comfortable, but 83% of our business comes to us through referrals. I think we should spend our extra resources on catering to our existing customers and capitalizing on that 83% of our business rather than pour it all into marketing and capitalizing on 17% of our business."

  - "This project won't start to pay off for another three years, and one of our competitors just filed for a patent on something very similar. I feel like we might be too far behind to catch up, and instead we could devote our time to our existing products and work on increasing their market share."

  - "We're pretty sure we can get another nine months out of our conveyor. I know we'll need to upgrade soon, but for now I think we should sit on the money and invest it in something more pressing."

- **Encourage anyone who doesn't like a new idea to draw comparisons between the change you're currently contemplating and similar changes in the past.** Again, the perspective that comes with experience is one of the most valuable assets people bring to the table. So invite your Older or more-experienced colleagues to think of any past experience that reminds them of the issue at hand. This is especially important to do with any of your Older workers who may have begun to take themselves out of the game, as it will simultaneously

---

[7] Nor do I want to beat a living horse. Or any horse for that matter. Why do people beat horses so much?

make them feel valued and force them to participate in the discussion. If they're able to come up with any comparisons from their previous experience, then you'll get some valuable insight about which direction you should go; and if they can't, then you'll be able to convince everyone that you're facing a relatively unique situation and need everyone's input in order to make your best educated guess about which course to take.

- **Expect to compromise.** Inevitably you'll hear sound arguments from both sides of the discussion, and you should make it clear that you plan to incorporate some of what you hear into the final version of your idea. However, because no amount of conversation can convince everyone that there's only one right answer to the problem at hand...

- **Accept the fact that you will rarely have enthusiastic support from 100% of the people involved.** No matter how well researched your new idea is, implementation will always involve some amount of risk, and it's very likely that some people will continue to think the risk isn't worth the potential reward. If you wait for 100% agreement, you'll be waiting forever. Sometimes the best thing to do is simply dive in and see what happens. After all, a real leader is someone who has a vision for how to proceed, incorporates the advice of others into that vision, and possesses the strength of will to execute that vision without knowing for certain whether his or her decisions are the right ones. You'll have plenty of opportunity for reflection and revision as you move forward, and you may make changes along the way. But you can't let that fear or the disagreement of others prevent you from acting when the time for action has come.

- **Admit mistakes when they occur.** Nobody's perfect—not even me. Which means that sometimes you'll have advocated for a new idea that will fail. Other times you'll insist on staying with a "proven" system that becomes cumbersome or unprofitable. When that happens, admit as much to the people who disagreed with your decision in the first place. It won't erase the mistake. But if you've done everything right, those people will both appreciate that you listened to their objections before implementation and respect that you were strong enough to admit your error.

Recognizing that our attitude toward specific changes is not a generational issue will go a long way toward helping you view your Younger or Older colleagues in a new light. They aren't intractable enemies, and they aren't so locked into a particular generational mindset that there's no hope of getting them to see things differently. They've simply chosen to focus on different things than you have— which means there *is* hope of getting them to see things your way, as long as you're patient and willing to explain it to them.

Fundamentally, all of us think the way we do things is right. As a result, we tend to think people who do things differently than we do are misguided at best and dangerously wrong at worst. This is true not only of generational differences but of religions, systems of government, approaches to marriage, attitudes toward exercise, and pretty much everything else. Because we more commonly identify with people our own age, we tend to believe that all Young People think one way, while all Old People think another. Because Older People have more reasons to be complacent than their Younger colleagues, and given today's Young People have only ever lived in a world defined by constant and rapid change, we tend to believe that Young People are universally impatient for change and Old People are universally opposed to it. Indeed, this "wisdom" is so prevalent that most generational books take it for granted as truth.

But as we've just pointed out, that isn't really true. When it comes to addressing specific changes, you will find people of all ages who are both excited and concerned. Moreover, you will also find people of all ages who will ultimately be proven right *and* wrong to have embraced a new idea, just as you will find people of all ages who will ultimately be proven right *and* wrong to have resisted a new idea. Unfortunately, although each of us thinks that the way we do things is right, that simply is not always the case.

That concept is so important to understand, in fact, that it's the bulk of what we discuss in the next chapter.

Key Strategies for Resolving Issues with Your Younger or Less-Experienced Colleagues

(reproduced from Chapters 4–6)

1. Present your new hires with business cards on their first day of work.

2. Invite your newest employees or team members to deliver a presentation to the rest of your team on a topic they already know something about.

3. Learn their names quickly, call them by name when you say hello, and praise them as often as you can think to.

4. If you are in a supervisory role, tell everyone who directly reports to you that you will go to bat for them if necessary.

5. Solicit the opinions of everyone who directly reports to you on a regular basis.

6. Invite your colleagues and employees to lunch on a weekly or monthly basis.

7. If you are a supervisor or manager, ask them what they want out of their jobs *over and above* the salary and benefits your company provides.

8. Offer your services as a mentor or create a mentorship program.

9. Give them the opportunity to use their skills and abilities on a regular basis.

10. If you have some young colleagues or employees with substandard work ethics, compare their careers to other common experiences they may be familiar with.

11. Share your own path to professional success with your young colleagues or employees.

12. Instill an appreciation for delayed gratification by presenting the impending retirement of your older workers as an opportunity for your younger workers.

13. Periodically highlight examples of people who succeeded after repeated failures or other setbacks.

14. Emphasize the similarities between professional and personal successes.

15. Point out, when applicable, that age and experience are not *always* correlated.

16. If necessary, fire your young employees quickly.

17. Explain to Young People *why* you do things the way you do.

18. Find examples to illustrate how all of us sometimes benefit from doing things the way we've always done them.

19. Use a previous failure to illustrate the occasional value of "business as usual."

20. Impress upon everyone the reality that change is occurring faster now than it used to.

21. Work every day to create a culture that actively opposes the urge toward complacency.

(Chapter 7)

22. **Be able to explain *specifically* how you believe a new initiative will improve business.**

23. **Be able to explain *specifically* how you believe sticking with an existing strategy is the best approach.**

24. **Encourage anyone who doesn't like a new idea to draw comparisons between the change you're currently contemplating and similar changes in the past.**

25. **Expect to compromise.**

26. **Accept the fact that you will rarely have enthusiastic support for your decision from 100% of the people involved.**

27. **Admit mistakes when they occur.**

Key Strategies for Resolving Issues with Your Older or More-Experienced Colleagues

(Reproduced from Chapters 4–6)

1. If you are in a supervisory role, tell everyone who directly reports to you that you will go to bat for them if necessary.

2. Solicit the opinions of everyone who directly reports to you on a regular basis.

3. Invite your colleagues and employees to lunch on a weekly or monthly basis.

4. Ask your colleagues and employees why they have stayed with your company as long as they have.

5. If you are a supervisor or manager, ask your colleagues and employees what they want out of their jobs *over and above* the salary and benefits your company provides.

6. Give your colleagues and employees the opportunity to use their skills and abilities on a regular basis.

7. Tell your manager or other senior employees that you intend to spend your career working your way up the ladder at your company.

8. Find an older or more-experienced person and ask him or her to be your mentor.

9. If you are younger or more inexperienced than most of your colleagues, make it clear that you are prepared to work hard.

10. Periodically highlight examples of people who succeeded after repeated failures or other setbacks.

11. Emphasize the similarities between professional and personal success.

12. Point out, when applicable, that age and experience are not *always* correlated.

13. If necessary, encourage your older employees into early retirement.

14. Remind change-averse people that they have been changing constantly throughout their entire personal and professional lives.

15. Impress upon everyone the reality that change is occurring faster now than it used to.

16. Work every day to create a culture that actively opposes the urge toward complacency.

(Chapter 7)

17. Be able to explain *specifically* how you believe a new initiative will improve business.

18. Be able to explain *specifically* how you believe sticking with an existing strategy is the best approach.

19. Encourage anyone who doesn't like a new idea to draw comparisons between the change you're currently contemplating and similar changes in the past.

20. Expect to compromise.

21. Accept the fact that you will rarely have enthusiastic support for your decision from 100% of the people involved.

22. Admit mistakes when they occur.

8

From Them to Us

In late 2013, the *Wall Street Journal* published an article called, "The Slowest Generation," whose mid-50s author excoriated Young People for not taking races seriously enough. Median marathon finish times rose by 44 minutes from 1980 to 2011, one of many facts the author used to accuse Young People of an endemic and increasing laziness.

The article irritated me, and so I wrote a reply. An abbreviated version is provided here.

The Unappeasable Generation: Old People Complain That Having Fun Is Akin to Communism

For the most part, I'm not particularly partisan when it comes to issues of generational supremacy. I'm 35, comfortably wedged between the Boomers and Millennials and thus incapable of deciding if I am actually a young or old person. I listen to modern music, and yet I write my texts in complete sentences. I live in a trendy downtown apartment where the owners have more dogs than kids, but I also occasionally write checks because I haven't gotten around to converting all my bills to auto-pay. I have an app for almost everything, but I still print my plane tickets because I'm worried my phone will die when I'm about to board. So I tend to take a "both sides are right" attitude to the argument about whether young people are better than old people or the other way around.

However, thanks to "The Slowest Generation," I know now where I belong, at least with respect to distance running. The author, Mr. Helliker, considers it a disgrace that finish times for marathons and triathlons across the United States are declining overall. To quote Toni Reavis, one of his sources, "This is emblematic of the state of America's competitiveness, and should be of concern to us all." According to Mr. Helliker, the fact that young people are running slowly is yet another example of this generation's overall apathy and general uselessness.

I've read my fair share of generational pieces. I agree with a lot of the prevailing sentiments with respect to the Millennials—kids who were raised and trained by Baby Boomers, by the way, a fact that most of the complainers conveniently choose not to mention. This younger generation has a tendency toward laziness, toward easy solutions and away from responsibility. But Mr. Helliker's article is such a study in myopic intolerance that I am today compelled to defend our youngest members of society against an aging population that seems more and more to be utterly incapable of being satisfied by anything their children and grandchildren do.

Mr. Helliker's primary complaint stems from the fact that while he finished in the top 15% of his age group (50–54), he finished in the top 11% overall. In his words, "Team Geriatric outperformed the field." This is undoubtedly true.

It's also undoubtedly irrelevant. In 2010 there were approximately 10,000 competitors in the Chicago Triathlon; in 1994, however, there were only 3,900. Over the past two decades, thousands more people have decided to participate, many of whom are not and will never become competitive runners in any other sense. Some of them are running with a friend, raising money for charity, or simply entering the field of competitive running for the first time with no further goal than to complete a race that most of the world thinks is too hard to even attempt. Considering how contemptuous old people typically are of a generation that often has trouble concentrating on anything longer than a Vine video, you would think the desire to finish a triathlon or marathon would be a point in their favor. Instead, however, the fact of increased participation is immediately subordinated to the greater concern that they are not finishing fast enough.

Which leads to Mr. Helliker's second major complaint: the rise of Color Runs, Tough Mudders, and other races that—horror of horrors—don't keep track of finish times. This is the real crime, that some people are running races with no loftier objective than to maybe enjoy themselves. This is where the younger generation gets compared to Communists. "How well is that everybody-gets-a-trophy mentality working in our schools?" asks Joe Desena, founder of Spartan Race and a firm believer in keeping track of finishing times.

This aggressive contempt is the reason I wrote this article. Because shocking as this may be to Mr. Helliker and his impossible-to-please cohort, it turns out that not everyone does everything for exactly the same reasons. I also have concerns about the youngest members of our society; I used to be a high school teacher, and the lack of work ethic in too many of my students was appalling. But to lambast them for having any reason for participating other than the desire to finish as quickly as possible is a crime of gross ignorance. Remember, this is a generation that is also criticized for not knowing how to form real relationships, for being more comfortable in online chatrooms than on actual dates. Instead, thousands of them are getting together with friends—with real live people!—to participate in an athletic event that takes hours to complete. Some of them are young mothers and fathers pushing strollers. What's wrong with those idiots? Don't they know the stroller is going to slow them down?

My father ran his first marathon three months before his 60th birthday. He did it in part as a bittersweet tribute to his own father, who died from a heart attack before reaching his own 60th birthday. He ran it with my youngest brother, and they finished in just under six hours, a pace barely above a brisk walk—a pathetic time, embarrassing, the kind of time that Mr. Helliker and his friends would be ashamed of. My youngest brother ran alongside my father for 26.2 miles, sacrificing the fame and glory and inevitable endorsement deals that would have come from finishing in the top 10% of his age bracket so that he could encourage my father when his will to finish started to fade. Two years later, that day is still among my father's favorite memories.

This should not be a difficult concept to grasp, but since it apparently is I'll say it in small and simple words: People do things for dozens of different reasons, and those reasons are not always the same as your own. You do not have to like everyone else's reasons. You can even try to encourage them to see the value of your own reasons. But the more things you find to complain about, the less interested they will become in trying to meet your impossibly high standards. When nothing you do can satisfy the person you're trying to please, eventually you give up. And you absolutely should.

There are occasions when life really is about the journey. That's something young people deal with regularly when they get stuck in traffic behind a squadron of old people driving 10 miles an hour below the speed limit—"Why hurry, it's a beautiful day, and the leaves are changing." And you know what? Sometimes they're right. Sometimes it would benefit all of us to take things a little slower, to think twice before posting a wicked comment online and watching our life get ruined by the pitiless caprice of the viral Internet. That's something young people are constantly being told they need to learn.

Apparently some older people need the same advice.

Then, in 2014, while in the initial stages of thinking about this book, I posted an article on LinkedIn that went viral, with more than 70,000 people reading it in the first 48 hours. Its success, in fact, is part of the reason that this book exists. Here's an edited version:

Seven Things Old People Do That You Should Too

So let's get one thing straight, Baby Boomers: You're not babies anymore. You're in your 50s, so stop lying to yourselves. And in case you forgot, it was your parents who did all the booming. Stop taking credit for their hard work.

That said, you're not quite the dinosaurs that young people sometimes make you out to be. It's true that old people have trouble programming their televisions, and it's also true that they invented disco and should never really be forgiven for that.

But it's also true that some of your approaches to life and work are way, way better than you sometimes get credit for. Here are seven of them.

- **Picking up the phone once in a while.** It's not just for taking pictures, young people, and I promise the person on the other end of the line can't actually eat you through the phone. I know it's scary to have to actually talk one-on-one to another human being person, but give it a shot sometime. You'll find out pretty quickly that it's actually a lot more efficient than sending 45 texts back and forth. And who knows? You might even enjoy having a real conversation for a change.

- **Sticking with something for more than five minutes.** I know you think you're a master at multitasking. All of us think so, regardless of age. However, all of us are wrong. It is impossible to do 4 things at once and do each of them as well as we would if we just did 1 at a time. Besides, it's a lot more relaxing to spend our mental energy focusing on 1 problem at a time than on 16. For example, old people tend not to text and drive. And you know what? They still manage to get where they're going, and I'm pretty sure they've never lost a business deal because they waited eight more minutes to reply to someone.

- **Writing something longer than four sentences.** Twitter is great for something, I'm sure, but it's not good for writing anything even as long as this paragraph. And texting is great for lots of things, but it's terrible for having any in-depth conversation. (If you've gotten into an argument via text because you forgot a smiley face or your auto-correct decided to screw with you, you'll know what I'm talking about.) Old people know this, which is why they still write emails and make phone calls. (Argh! There's that stupid phone call thing again!)

- **Picking one or two hobbies at a time and sticking to them.** My grandfather played golf and collected stamps. (He also drank scotch, but since you can do that while playing golf and collecting stamps, I'm not counting it as a separate hobby.) Your grandparents probably have one or two things they really enjoy doing. And the reason they don't have more is because they know you can't really get good at something if you don't spend a good amount of time on it. If you've joined 43 kickball leagues and trivia nights and networking groups—or, worse, if you're trying to manage 14 social media accounts—then all you're really doing is failing to excel at any of them. If you'll notice, most billionaires are extremely good at a very narrow range of business skills—high finance, commercial real estate,

SEO, whatever. Sometimes, when it comes to being successful, less really is more.

- **Knowing when to stop growing their beards.** There are still a few holdout hippies, but most old people have a solid understanding of the difference between "distinguished beard" and "I think that man might kill me." Young people, I beg you, stop making me wonder if you're about to kill me. I know I should be open-minded and all that, and I know it's your turn to re-create the heady days of the early '60s that your parents pioneered, but it's just...so...much...beard!!!!!

- **Writing thank-you notes.** After her first interview, my wife wrote 26 thank-you notes to everyone who interviewed her. (It was an absurdly thorough process.) She did it because old people told her she should. Fortunately, we had a lot of wine on hand, because by the end of it, she was pretty much over the whole thing. But you know what? She got the job. That's not the only reason, of course—she also happens to be awesome and have great taste in men. But it definitely didn't hurt.

- **Marching to other people's drummers.** I know that doing so is an affront to the very freedom on which this country was founded. But you know what? That freedom was won by soldiers, who absolutely marched to another person's drummer. I mean literally there was a drummer there, and they all marched to whatever beat he played. Sometimes "taking one for the team" isn't a sacrifice; it's a strategy for ultimately getting where you want to be.

There. I hope this makes the old people you work with seem at least a little more useful than they did otherwise. They don't have all the best ideas, but they do have some of them. If you write them off, all they'll do is write you off in return. And they absolutely should.

We've come a long way from where we started. We've discussed eight key concepts that Young People and Old People have in common, as well as several explanations for why your Younger or Older colleagues think and behave the way they do. You've been given a couple dozen strategies to address generational issues with people significantly Older or more-experienced than you, as well as a couple dozen to address people significantly Younger or less experienced. For your convenience, those have all been compiled in Chapters 12, "Summary of Main Points," and 13, "Summary of Strategies."

However, that might all seem a bit overwhelming. And because the point of this book is to make things simple, I want to mention that you don't have to do each and every one of the strategies you've been given—these are just some of your options. Also if this feels like too much, focus on just the key concepts. Understand them, and the right strategies will come to you naturally.

But I want to try to simplify things even further. Twitter has done that, and it's made a ton of money. So let's see if I can knock each concept down to 140 characters:

- **Loyalty must be earned and can't be assumed.** This is true in every type of human relationship, personal and professional. If you are not working to create a loyal environment, you will not have loyal workers. If you are not willing to be a loyal team player, you will not receive the benefits that loyalty would earn you.

- **Advancement is an unending process, not an inalienable right.** Everything you're good at today—every single thing, including the things you had a natural inclination for—is a result of practice, dedication, and perseverance. Remember this and don't expect to be given something you've made no concentrated effort to earn or to keep something you make no concentrated effort to maintain.

- **Existing business practices exist for very good reasons.** This does not mean they can't be modernized or updated, but it does mean that (a) they represent the best ideas anyone at your company has ever had, and (b) barring an imminent crisis, they are the best starting point for figuring out how to modernize. The past informs the future—it always has, and it still does.

- **Questions and ideas are not an implicit attack on existing systems or your own authority.** Some existing practices are outdated, and others could be improved. That is not your fault and should not be interpreted as a weakness; it is simply a function of the fact that things change.

- **New ideas are inherently risky, and you can't perfectly predict which will succeed and which will fail.** Some will become embarrassing mistakes, and others will lead to wild success. The only way you can minimize the former and maximize the latter is to talk about all new ideas long enough to make the most well-informed decisions you possibly can.

- **Some things move at a different speed than you wish they did.** This is not my opinion; it's simply the way of the world. Career advancement happens relatively slowly, and technological advancement happens relatively quickly. If that's not entirely to your liking, take comfort in the fact that it's not entirely to anyone's liking. At least we're all in the same boat.

Once again, you'll notice that I've moved away from framing these issues as "generational." That's because the core difficulties we face have nothing to do with generational qualities and everything to do with perspective. The big problem is that Young People do not have the ability to see the world the same way Old People do because they haven't lived long enough to experience the same things, and Old People typically forget what it's like to think like a Young Person because that's just what happens.

This is an important point: The people you work with who occupy different generations than yours are not fundamentally different than you. They aren't operating under a completely new and heretofore unknown system of human behavior. They are simply at a different stage in their lives and careers than you. If they're Older or more experienced than you are, then they're doing what you (or at least some of your same-age colleagues) will do once you reach their age and experience level. And if they're Younger or less experienced than you are, then they're doing what you (or at least some of your same-age colleagues) did at their age—they're looking at the world they've inherited and deciding how best to make a difference and how best to get what they want. The conditions may be different today than they were 50 years ago, and the technology is certainly different than it was 30 years ago. But *people* are not fundamentally different today than they have been since the beginning of human civilization. Once again, we are all far more Us than Them. The more you see your colleagues as people, and the more you can imagine how you would behave if you were in their positions, the more smoothly your business will run.

But I said I was going to try to knock this all down into a Twitter post, and I obviously failed at that. If this were a YouTube video, you would have already switched over to the next video. So I'll try again: Young People, you don't know how to think like your Older or more-experienced colleagues because you simply haven't lived the same experiences they have. Old People, you've mostly forgotten how to think like your Younger or less-experienced colleagues because time and distance make it virtually impossible to remember how we felt 5, 10, 20, and 50 years ago. I think we can all agree on that.

So here is your Twitter takeaway, your one-sentence summary of generational differences in the workplace of yesterday, today, tomorrow, and 1,000 years from now:

No matter what generation you are a part of, you do not know everything there is to know.

That's it. That's all there is to say. You do not know everything there is to know. That's the reason we hire consultants, talk to marriage counselors, listen to TED talks, and read business books. This entire book has been an attempt to illustrate this single concept. All the statistics and examples and psychological explanations and various anecdotes have brought us here. No one group of people has a monopoly on knowledge, and *all* of the generational issues you've faced or will face at work are direct results of people thinking they understand more than they actually do.

Here's a softer way of looking at this: No one group of people knows *everything*. I deliver presentations for a living—hundreds of cities, 49 states, 2 countries, and counting. I've spoken at tech conferences, agricultural expos, health care summits, women's business symposia, bankers' associations, government agencies, nonprofits, sales conferences, hospitality conventions, and everything in between. I've met rich people, poor people, hard-line conservatives, hard-line liberals, urbanites, country folk, capitalists, quasi-anarchists, immigrants, and every other group of people imaginable. And I can say with *perfect* confidence that if any one of those groups of people were suddenly endowed with the ability to impose their will on the rest of us, our world would take an immediate turn for the worse. If the United States were run entirely by uncompromising Republicans or uncompromising Democrats, the United States probably wouldn't still exist. If your marriage is dominated entirely, in every decision, by the wishes of only one of you, you have an unhealthy marriage. As much as it pains me to admit this, it turns out that other people occasionally have good ideas.

Young People, you *need* the Old People you work with to teach you patience, to give you perspective, and to show you what they've done and how they've done it. Without them and the benefit of their advice, you'll end up wasting an enormous amount of time trying to reinvent the wheel—a wheel that you're not likely to reinvent any better than they've already invented it. To help drive this point home: Mark Zuckerberg founded Facebook, Larry Page and Sergey Brin founded Google, Steve Jobs founded Apple, and Bill Gates founded Microsoft, and all of them did it before they were 30, but *none* of them did it without listening to the advice of a whole lot of Old People who knew a whole lot more about running businesses than they did.

Old People, you *need* the Young People you work with to look at your business with fresh eyes, to ask questions that are difficult to answer, and to help you navigate the world at the speed at which it moves today. Because they were born into a hyperactive world, today's Young People are masters at holding onto to ideas for only as long as they're useful and then happily switching to whatever new, seemingly better thing comes next. They've been doing it their entire lives, and it's a skill all of us can learn from them.

In His Own Words: R. Li on Working Together

We first met R. Li in Chapter 4. He's the 67-year-old Baby Boomer whose career trajectory came nowhere close to following a straight line. Here's what he had to say about his experiences working with people from different generations:

> Throughout my working life, I've worked for older and younger bosses. I've also managed younger and older employees. In most cases, a mutual respect allowed for a good working relationship, whether I was the employee or the boss. However, when egos battled, reason and balance were lost, and tension gripped the working environment.

I want to end this chapter with one final observation. When you really get down to it, the entire conversation about generational differences in the workplace is somewhat misleading. The issues we've discussed throughout this book—loyalty, work ethic, change management, expectations of career advancement, and so on—are issues rooted primarily in our attitude and experience. There are people of all ages who are naturally loyal, perennially lazy, devoted workaholics, chronically impatient, exuberant risk-takers, instinctively conservative, methodical, chaotic, and every other combination of qualities that it is possible for people to have.

Indeed, the most common criticism people have about any previous attempt to define a given generation is that the descriptions don't perfectly match. And that's true—they don't, because they can't. There is no quality or characteristic that we can attribute entirely to people in their 30s or 50s or to people who are exactly 6 months into their professional lives or 3 years away from retirement. Each of us is a unique combination of our particular experiences, which in turn shape our beliefs about life and work. All of us come from different backgrounds with different desires, upbringings, mentors, cultural influences, and educational experiences—and *all* of that plays a role in shaping who we become, what we want out of our lives, and how hard we're willing to work in order to get it.

Because of this, the only way to perfectly address the problem of bringing everyone you work with into the Us camp is as follows: Get to know everyone you work with so thoroughly that you can provide exactly the kind of incentives, encouragement, recognition, and opportunities they are looking for.[1] Anything less than this is necessarily imperfect and will therefore fall short of the ideal working environment we're all striving to create. However, this strategy is at best impractical and most likely completely impossible.

Thus, we are forced to find ways to try to simplify what would otherwise be a superhuman task. Some authors and experts have chosen to use personality types as their framework for understanding how we work together. It's a good approach, given that our personalities

---

[1] This is also the core strategy of the vast majority of any leadership, communication, and team-building book you will ever read.

tend not to change very much; that is, an introvert usually stays intro-verted throughout his or her entire life. However, theirs is also an imperfect system, considering nobody is 100% introverted, analytical, emotional, or anything else. Still, viewing the human element of your business as a collection of discrete personality types makes a certain amount of sense, as long as the number of "types" is small enough to understand and manage. A personality test designed to distill your workforce into 23 separate categories would hardly simplify the way you interact with others or encourage them to perform at higher levels. I'm certain that those who focus on personality types have done everything they can to distill the entirety of humanity into as few personality types as they can specifically in order to make their system as practical as possible. It is the same reason I advocate for a two-generation model.

One of the reasons it makes sense to divide the working world along generational lines (vs. personality types) is that many of our attitudes change with time and experience, and those changes have a bearing on how we act. Because loyalty requires time to develop and thrive, it's generally true that people become more loyal as they get older. It's also true that people tend toward complacency as they age because the pressure to innovate and change decreases incre-mentally as we develop a track record of success. Youth often agitates for change because we yearn to prove ourselves and be taken seri-ously as we mature, and there is no better way for the young to make that happen than to force their elders to admit the merit of their own actions and ideas. The things that motivate us also tend to change as we get older; all of us generally crave meaning and purpose more than money when we're young, and all of us slowly evolve as we put down roots and start families and realize that we have more to think about than just ourselves and our own goals.

But again, these are just *tendencies*, not absolutes. We humans are complicated, and as we try to deal with one another, often the best we can hope for is to think in ways that simplify those complications as best as possible. That's what I have attempted to do here. I believe very strongly that this two-generation, Us vs. Them, approach is a simpler—and thus more effective—way to look at generational issues than the four-generation model we've been hearing about for so long.

I hope you'll agree. But even if you don't, I hope you've found something in this book that you can use.

Correction: I hope you use the something in this book that you found. (Sorry, I got the words out of order in that last paragraph.) And to help make sure you're able to apply this information in a productive way, make sure to check out Part Three. My editors made me include a third section because they argued (quite convincingly, I might add) that things with three parts are better than things with two. They pointed out that *The Lord of the Rings* would have been awfully depressing if it had ended with *The Two Towers*, and if our fingers had only two parts, then we'd each have 10 thumbs, and that would look weird.

Part Three is short, awesome, and short. In it you'll find all of the key concepts and strategies we've discussed throughout this book, along with some concrete steps for having successful conversations with people who are significantly Older or more experienced or Younger or less experienced than you are. Along the way we also shatter the idiotic notion that Baby Boomers are universally "live to work" automatons while everyone younger than them is a "work to live" vagabond. There might be some other things in there too, but if I give it all away right now, then you'll have less incentive to read it for yourself.

So please, don't make me do all your work for you. Haven't we discussed enough the importance of working hard? Turn the page already!

Part Three
Key Concepts and Strategies

9

How to Talk to Someone Significantly Older or More Experienced Than You Are

So you're stuck working with a bunch of Old People. It was probably too much to hope that they would hire you and then immediately retire *en masse*, but having that dream fail to materialize is nevertheless disappointing. It's not that you have a problem with Old People. Far from it: You know plenty of delightful Old People, and your grandparents have been buying your love for years with that check they send every birthday. It's that your new colleagues *act* old, playing it so safe that you wouldn't be surprised to see training wheels on their weird recumbent bicycles. They wouldn't know a brilliant new idea if it smacked them in the face. You're certain of that; you've been trying to smack them since day one, and they haven't even blinked.

Unfortunately, you're going to be stuck with them for a while. Too many of them have failed to save properly for retirement, and anyway they're so married to their jobs that they don't know what they'd do with themselves if they had too much free time. And with all the recent advances in medicine, they might be working right next to you for forever.

You're welcome to hate these people for the rest of your career. You can complain to your friends about their stodgy ways and shake your head at their stubborn refusal to acknowledge your genius. You can rail against the gross injustice of not being able to run your company five months into your career, and you can excoriate your elders for conspiring in secret to keep you out of the most important conversations. If you wish to work forever in a self-imposed exile, that's your right.

But in case you want to earn the respect you're undoubtedly demanding, this chapter describes a step-by-step process to help you bridge the gap between yourself and anyone significantly Older or more experienced than you are.

Step 1: Expect Some Condescension from Them

Nine times out of ten, it won't be intentional. Yes, you'll run across the occasional know-it-all braggart, but you can find those people everywhere from age 8 to 88. For the vast majority of your Older colleagues, however, any skepticism or disdain you think they're throwing at you will be the accidental byproduct of their experience. They like the way they do things because they've found success with those strategies, and they're not immediately going to see any need to do anything differently. Neither would you in their position, and neither *do* you when someone significantly Younger than you suggests you should change the way you do things. If you interpret their attitude as an attack on you and your ideas, you'll be setting yourself up for a fight. If instead you realize that they don't mean to make you feel inferior or unappreciated, you'll be prepared to establish a strong relationship.

Step 2: Let Them Do Most of the Talking

At least do this at first. Your turn will come. But unless you've been hired because of your particular expertise, you have to accept your role as the student. If you allow them to, most of your Older colleagues will be happy to talk about what they do and why they do it that way, partially to initiate you into your company's culture and partially because all of us like talking about things we understand very well. Establishing yourself as a willing listener is a critical element of any successful relationship, and there will be plenty of time for the inevitable questions and ideas you'll be stockpiling while you learn how things currently function.

Step 3: Praise Anything You Hear That Sounds Intelligent

If you've ever tried teaching a child to play the piano, then you know how frustrating it is to go through a painstaking explanation of chords and scales and melodies only to watch the child ignore everything you've said and play whack-a-mole with the keys. In exactly the same way, your Older colleagues will be frustrated if you listen to their explanations about how and why they do things only to start in with your own "new and better" approach. If you can't find something reasonable, intelligent, shrewd, or eye-opening in the way your company currently operates, then you either haven't been paying attention or you've been hired into the wrong company. The second you let your Older colleagues know that you value what they've done, they'll be prepared to listen to you. Just don't take this one too far, or you might come off like a brainless brown-noser.

Step 4: Ask a Lot of Questions

If you understand the way your business works and have some ideas about how to improve it, there are basically two ways to go about it: by telling or by asking. Starting out with "I have an idea," implies that you've come up with a foolproof solution to the wealth of inefficiencies your Older colleagues are too blind to see—and it will probably make them slightly defensive. Instead, try something like, "Why are we still advertising on mainstream radio?" or "Has anyone ever conducted a focus group with Latin American families?" This way you can introduce your ideas under the guise of trying to more fully understand how things work. It feels slower, but it will work better—and more quickly—than trying to start at the finish line.

Step 5: Expect Some Frustration

Eventually, if you ask enough questions, you'll get some pushback. If your Older colleagues are comfortable with the way they do things, they won't enjoy the implication that there's something wrong with it. And neither would you, so don't expect them to be happy with all of your suggestions. The process of consciously incorporating new ideas into our existing framework is always a bumpy one. If you get mad at your Older or more-experienced colleagues for not immediately embracing the wisdom of whatever it is you're saying, you'll accomplish nothing.

Step 6: Focus on Improving the Business

Finally, you can act. If you've taken all five other steps, you've positioned yourself as attentive, thoughtful, and appreciative of many of your Older colleagues' ideas, and you've also asked enough questions that it's clear you have some ideas of your own. If your 51-year-old team lead is dead set on ignoring everything you have to say, take your ego out of it. Don't focus on it being *your* idea; focus on the fact that the idea could save money, eliminate redundancy, or reduce stress. If you've asked questions your Older colleagues didn't know how to answer, point out that their inability to do so is basically the same as admitting that there is a problem (or an opportunity). And if they *still* don't listen, find different Older colleagues and repeat the entire process until you get one of them on board. Everything is easier with allies. Is it fun when a 61-year-old chooses only to listen to other 61-year-olds? No, but don't worry. Everyone will know where the idea came from. Your ego will have its day.

Talking with someone significantly older or more experienced doesn't have to difficult. It just becomes difficult sometimes because we want things to happen faster than they are likely to. Trust me, I also wish you could start the New York Marathon at mile 25. But I've tried, and the police there are just not accommodating.

10

How to Talk to Someone Significantly Younger or Less Experienced Than You Are

Alas, you probably work with some Young People. Your company, in its depressingly finite wisdom, gave these children a chance to play at being grown-ups. They haven't been working for very long—a couple years maybe, possibly even less—and their inexperience offends you. They think they know *everything*, when in fact their ignorance of how things really work is so vast they should be constantly embarrassed by it. But nothing embarrasses them, does it? They could trip over their absurdly bushy beards and fall face-down in the atrium of your building, and they'd probably just take a selfie of it and post it to their social media sites before bothering to stand up.

However, in all likelihood, you're going to be stuck with them for a while. Young People have the supremely annoying habit of not recognizing when they're not wanted, and many of them have fallen prey to the siren call of a paycheck and the things it allows them to purchase. They'll be working right next to you until the siren call of retirement becomes too powerful for you to resist any longer.

Now you're welcome to hate these people for the rest of your career. You can roll your eyes at their misplaced enthusiasm, grumble about their idiotic ideas, and seethe quietly as they consistently fail to talk about their minor aches and pains. You can exclude them from sitting at your lunch table and accidentally forget to invite them to happy hour after work. If you wish to end your professional career as a semi-recluse, it's completely within your power to do so.

But in case you want to act like the grown-up you've pretended to be for so long, this chapter describes a step-by-step process to help you bridge the gap between yourself and anyone significantly Younger or less experienced than you are.

Step 1: Expect Some Impatience from Them

Young People have forever been impatient, and new employees—especially good ones—are naturally eager to prove themselves. This is a quality you had as well when you were their age, although most of us eventually forget that we were ever impulsive and headstrong 22-year-olds. ("Surely I wasn't *this* bad!" Yes, you were. So was I.) If you expect your inexperienced juniors to behave with the calm temperance that is really only honed in the crucible of experience, you'll only end up frustrated. If you accept their impatience as a natural quality of youth, you'll be better able to address and ultimately change it.

Step 2: Temper Their Impatience by Showing Them Why They Need to Slow Down

Young People will not enter their professional lives with an instinctive understanding of how your culture and processes operate, so you'll need to show them. There are several ways to do this—for example, explaining your own path of career advancement and highlighting how long it took to go from where you began to where you are now; explaining why your sales cycle takes as long as it does or why design specs need to be reviewed five times instead of two; explaining why it took three years to fully overhaul your intranet—and you should do all of them as often as you can think to do so. You'll notice a lot of explaining on your end, and there's really no way around that. If you wait for them to figure it all out on their own, you'll both end up frustrated at how long it's taking. The more you explain, the less pushback you'll get from them about the way things currently work.

Step 3: Expect Them to Become Frustrated and Empathize with Them

As soon as any of us realizes that something is going to take longer than we thought it would, we all tend to get frustrated. (If you don't believe me, try making it through a major home improvement project sometime without cursing at a single one of the unexpected problems that will surely pop up.) This means your Younger and less-experienced colleagues will almost certainly view your attempt to reign in their expectations with some irritation. This is natural, and you've felt the same way yourself. So let them know you understand their frustration and that you've felt it too. Will it completely eliminate their frustration? Of course not. But it should calm them down enough to listen to reason.

Step 4: Point Out the Positive Elements of Every Idea Before Focusing on the Negative Elements

If a Younger colleague is complaining about the antiquated nature of one of your existing processes, you'll get a lot farther by first highlighting the various benefits to using it than you will by railing at the complainer for having a problem in the first place. Similarly, if a new hire comes to you with an idea that you think is ridiculous or impractical, finding *anything* good about it will make the conversation smoother than a knee-jerk rejection.

Step 5: Point Out the Potential Problems

At this point you've told your Younger colleagues what they should expect, empathized with their frustration, and stoked their egos by acknowledging the merits of their own way of thinking. Now it's time to highlight drawbacks, which means suggesting that their "great new idea" hasn't been thought through quite as perfectly as they originally thought or that your own approach might also leave something to be desired. If you've done step 4 already, this should play out more as a conversation than an argument, which I assume is what you're going for.

Step 6: Empower Your Young or Inexperienced Colleague to Address the Issues Brought Up in Step 5

Now it's time for action. If your inexperienced colleague is hell-bent on pursuing her great new idea, encourage her to do so once she's figured out how to address your thoughtful and considered objections to it. If some punk 23-year-old has listened to everything you've said and still thinks it's unfair that he hasn't been promoted 6 months into his career, push him to come up with a plan for accelerated career advancement others can get on board with. You'll be putting all the responsibility on him, which will probably please both of you. If he does what you've suggested, he'll be demonstrating an admirable dedication to a cause and may end up devising a fantastic solution (although you might have to repeat steps 4–6 a few times). And if he doesn't do it, then you'll be able to point that out to him the next time he starts complaining, which should shut him up for a while.

Talking with someone significantly Younger or less experienced doesn't have to be difficult. It just becomes difficult sometimes because we expect everyone to behave exactly like we do. Trust me, I wish everyone did exactly what I wanted them to. But if that were the case, I might not have a job anymore. Hmmm.

11

How Our Motivations Change as We Age

When it comes to generational differences in the workplace, one of the most common distinctions made between the generations is that Traditionalists and Baby Boomers "live to work," while Gen Xers and Millennials "work to live." This is typically presented as a generation-specific quality; in other words, Baby Boomers have always lived to work, and Millennials will always work to live. Nothing could be further from the truth, and correcting this misperception will go a long way toward bridging a generational divide that often seems intractable.

Think of "work to live" and "live to work" as occupying opposite ends of a straight line. At one end, we have the pure "work to live" person, who does only what he or she must in order to get what he or she *wants*. At the other end, the perfect "live to work" person does whatever is necessary to get what he or she *needs*.

In this envisioning, the typical professional career starts closer to the "work to live" side of the line and moves progressively toward the latter—regardless of age, or culture, or generational indoctrination. This is simply what happens, and it happens because of the fairly predictable way in which the majority of us change as we age.

When we leave high school or college and first enter the professional world, most of us owe allegiance only to ourselves. Most of us aren't married and don't have mortgages or children, which means we are free to concentrate on our own desires. For this reason, most Young People operate with a "work to live" mentality. This is absolutely not a Millennial quality, although Millennials might inhabit this mentality longer than previous generations because they are typically waiting longer to buy homes, get married, and have children.

But nobody in the 1960s—literally *nobody*—would have classified 20-something Baby Boomers as a "live to work" group of people.

However, the vast majority of us accumulate various duties and responsibilities as we age. We purchase homes and boats and rental properties and obligate ourselves to make enough money to support those purchases; we get married and have children and suddenly start thinking about the costs of college education and all the other desires our spouse and children might have for themselves. This is a natural process, and most of us enter into it willingly. And as we realize that we are no longer living our lives entirely on our own terms, we become more and more "live to work" people. We can fight against this if we choose, and plenty of people have decided not to allow their careers to completely dictate every facet of their lives. But there is no getting around the fact that the typical married homeowner is more "live to work" than her single, apartment-renting friend.

That's not to say this must be a one-way process. Sometimes we shed responsibilities—find a less stressful job, get divorced, sell our expensive and burdensome vacation home—and that gives us a chance to return to a more "work to live" lifestyle. The most common incarnation of this typically happens near the end of our careers, when the kids are out of the house and our mortgage is ideally paid off. Then we opt for early retirement or decide not to fight for that next promotion—not because we don't care about working hard but because we've decided we don't need to push as hard as we had to in the past. Obviously, this isn't true for everyone, but it is an easily recognizable trend.

In fact, it's the exceptions that prove the rule. There are endless examples of 20-year-old "live to work" single parents, or never-married 46-year-old "work to live" playboys, or 64-year-olds with unemployed children who have no intention of relaxing their way into retirement because their reality precludes that option. We all know people who don't fit the generational mold that's been handed to us—so why do we keep repeating this "work-to-live/live-to-work" dichotomy as though it's somehow dependent upon the year in which we were born?

Bottom line: If you're trying to unravel the motivations that govern your workforce, do yourself a favor. Ignore whatever convenient (and useless) generational labels you've been given and instead pay attention to what stage of life people are currently in. Doing so will almost certainly tell you more about their attitude toward work, life, and the balance between them than anything else.

12

Summary of Main Points

1. All of us, regardless of age or station, want to be loyal to someone or something.

2. All of us, regardless of age or station, want others to be loyal to us.

3. All of us become more or less loyal based on our experiences. When we can point to concrete instances in which our loyalty has been repaid, we slowly and steadily become more loyal. When we feel as though our loyalty is not being valued, we become slowly and steadily less loyal. In other words, all of us believe that loyalty is something that needs to be earned and can't simply be assumed.

4. All of us are struggling to find reasons to be loyal to our employers because all of us have seen too many instances in which the major incentives that foster loyalty are being taken away.

5. All of us get better at things slowly and steadily over time. This is true for absolutely everything we do, both professionally and personally.

6. All of us, Young People as well as Old People, sometimes forget the truth of the statement above.

7. Change is the natural state, and all of us are constantly incorporating countless changes into our daily lives, both personal and professional. None of us is the same person we were a year ago, and none of us will be the same person a year from now.

With respect to our professional selves, none of us is working in exactly the same way as we were a year ago, and none of us will be working exactly the same way a year from today.

8. As we experience success or avoid failure, all of us naturally look for ways to replicate that success or continue to prevent that failure. As a result, all of us tend to become complacent with the way we are currently doing things.

Key Concepts: Why Your Younger or Less-Experienced Colleagues Think and Behave the Way They Do

1. Today's Young People are actually more interested in building loyal relationships than the Young People of previous generations, in part because they have grown up in a hyperconnected world in which an overload of options has made it more difficult to find and establish a position for themselves. Consequently, they are actively searching for people, companies, and ideas to which they can be loyal.

2. Today's Young People have only ever lived in a time in which the incentives that foster employee loyalty are disappearing, and many of them are wary and skeptical of their employers as a result.

3. Young People have not been working for as long as their Older colleagues and so have had less time to determine whether their loyalty to their company will be rewarded.

4. Many Young People mistakenly believe that because technology has accelerated virtually everything we do, it must necessarily accelerate the pace at which we acquire skills and knowledge. This mistake can be easily corrected by pointing to the process by which they themselves have developed proficiency in anything they consider themselves to be proficient at.

5. Some Young People are more experienced than their age would suggest and expect to be judged based on that experience.

6. Some Young People simply do not have a strong work ethic, either because they are naturally lazy or because they have been raised in a culture that rewarded them regardless of their ability or effort.

7. Because Young People have comparatively little experience with the benefits of your existing practices and processes, they are more likely to downplay or dismiss the value of those practices and processes.

8. Today's Young People tend to expect changes to occur relatively quickly, often in part because they have only ever lived in a world of constant, rapid change. As a result, Young People will tend to agitate for change more often and more quickly than their Older or more-experienced colleagues—not necessarily because they think current practices are failing but because constant change is the only speed they've been trained to understand.

Key Concepts: Why Your Older or More-Experienced Colleagues Think and Behave the Way They Do

1. Because they have been working for a longer period of time, Old People have had more opportunity to recognize that their loyalty will be rewarded and reciprocated.

2. Today's Old People grew up in a time when employee loyalty was more commonly rewarded, and many of them are still operating with that framework firmly embedded in their minds.

3. Old People have been going through the process of advancement longer than Young People, and for that reason they expect to be respected for the work they have done up to this point.

4. Some Old People no longer have the solid work ethic that has carried them from the beginning of their careers until now, either because they've become destructively complacent or because they believe they can skate by with relatively little effort.

5. Because Old People have experienced the benefits of your existing practices and processes, they are *more* likely to value those practices and processes and *less* likely to see the need to replace them with an untested approach.

6. Because complacency is a function of time, experience, and repetition, Old People are at greater risk of falling into complacent behaviors than their Younger counterparts.

13

Summary of Strategies

1. Present your new hires with business cards on their first day of work.

2. Invite your newest employees or team members to deliver a presentation to the rest of your team on a topic they already know something about.

3. Learn their names quickly, call them by name when you say hello, and praise them as often as you can think to.

4. If you are in a supervisory role, tell everyone who directly reports to you that you will go to bat for them if necessary.

5. Solicit the opinions of everyone who directly reports to you on a regular basis.

6. Invite your colleagues and employees to lunch on a weekly or monthly basis.

7. If you are a supervisor or manager, ask them what they want out of their jobs *over and above* the salary and benefits your company provides.

8. Offer your services as a mentor or create a mentorship program.

9. Give Young People the opportunity to use their skills and abilities on a regular basis.

10. If you have some Young colleagues or employees with substandard work ethics, compare their careers to other common experiences they may be familiar with.

11. Share your own path to professional success with your young colleagues or employees.

12. Instill an appreciation for delayed gratification by presenting the impending retirement of your Older workers as an opportunity for your Younger workers.

13. Periodically highlight examples of people who succeeded after repeated failures or other setbacks.

14. Emphasize the similarities between professional and personal successes.

15. Point out, when applicable, that age and experience are not *always* correlated.

16. If necessary, fire your Young employees quickly.

17. Explain to Young People *why* you do things the way you do.

18. Find examples to illustrate how all of us sometimes benefit from doing things the way we've always done them.

19. Use a previous failure to illustrate the occasional value of "business as usual."

20. Impress upon everyone the reality that change is occurring faster now than it used to.

21. Work every day to create a culture that actively opposes the urge toward complacency.

22. Be able to explain *specifically* how you believe a new initiative will improve business.

23. Be able to explain *specifically* how you believe sticking with an existing strategy is the best approach.

24. Encourage anyone who doesn't like a new idea to draw comparisons between the change you're currently contemplating and similar changes in the past.

25. Expect to compromise.

26. Accept the fact that you will rarely have enthusiastic support for your decision from 100% of the people involved.

27. Admit mistakes when they occur.

Key Strategies for Resolving Issues with Your Older or More-Experienced Colleagues

1. If you are in a supervisory role, tell everyone who directly reports to you that you will go to bat for them if necessary.

2. Solicit the opinions of everyone who directly reports to you on a regular basis.

3. Invite your colleagues and employees to lunch on a weekly or monthly basis.

4. Ask your colleagues and employees why they have stayed with your company as long as they have.

5. If you are a supervisor or manager, ask your colleagues and employees what they want out of their jobs *over and above* the salary and benefits your company provides.

6. Give your colleagues and employees the opportunity to use their skills and abilities on a regular basis.

7. Tell your manager or other senior employees that you intend to spend your career working your way up the ladder at your company.

8. Find an Older or more-experienced person and ask him or her to be your mentor.

9. If you are Younger or more inexperienced than most of your colleagues, make it clear that you are prepared to work hard.

10. Periodically highlight examples of people who succeeded after repeated failures or other setbacks.

11. Emphasize the similarities between professional and personal success.

12. Point out, when applicable, that age and experience are not *always* correlated.

13. If necessary, encourage your Older employees into early retirement.

14. Remind change-averse people that they have been changing constantly throughout their entire personal and professional lives.

15. Impress upon everyone the reality that change is occurring faster now than it used to.

16. Work every day to create a culture that actively opposes the urge toward complacency.

17. Be able to explain *specifically* how you believe a new initiative will improve business.

18. Be able to explain *specifically* how you believe sticking with an existing strategy is the best approach.

19. Encourage anyone who doesn't like a new idea to draw comparisons between the change you're currently contemplating and similar changes in the past.

20. Expect to compromise.

21. Accept the fact that you will rarely have enthusiastic support for your decision from 100% of the people involved.

22. Admit mistakes when they occur.

Index